42 Rules for Building a High-Velocity Inside Sales Team

Actionable Guide to Creating Inside Sales Teams that Deliver Quantum Results

By Lori L. Harmon and Debbi S. Funk

E-mail: info@superstarpress.com
20660 Stevens Creek Blvd., Suite 210
Cupertino, CA 95014

Published by Super Star Press™, a THiNKaha® imprint
20660 Stevens Creek Blvd., Suite 210, Cupertino, CA 95014
http://42rules.com

First Printing: January 2014
Paperback ISBN: 978-1-60773-115-3 (1-60773-115-0)
eBook ISBN: 978-1-60773-116-0 (1-60773-116-9)
Place of Publication: Silicon Valley, California, USA
Library of Congress Number: 2013956413

Trademarks

Warning and Disclaimer

Praise for This Book

"Lori and Debbi prove that they know how to build a high-velocity inside sales team. They make it clear that building an inside sales team is not a one-size-fits-all process. Although every team has to have some common key elements like tools, systems, and processes, it takes a strategic approach to put it together and build a successful team."
John Stringer, CEO, Producers Forum, Former CEO, Wyse Technology

"Inside sales is a category that a few years ago did not exist. Now the hiring of inside sales reps versus outside sales is 10:1. In order to build an inside sales team properly, you need to know how. 42 Rules for Building a High-Velocity Inside Sales Team outlines the process that will enable you to create a competitive differentiator that will deliver revenue and value to your company significantly faster than traditional sales models."
Lars Leckie, Managing Partner, Hummer Winblad

"I have found it extremely important to coach, inspire, and mentor your employees to maximize their individual success and that of the team. In 42 Rules for Building a High-Velocity Inside Sales Team, Lori and Debbi do a great job coaching managers through building a high-velocity inside sales team. They point out the importance of taking the time to work with individual reps to help each of them achieve their career goals."
Robert Fioretti, Business/Success Coach, Co-author, Discover Your Inner Strength, Keynote Speaker and Owner of Infinite Possibilities LLC

"In today's economy, innovation isn't just for products; it extends to your distribution model. Inside sales is leading the way in terms of innovation and breaking the traditional sales rules. 42 Rules for Building a High-Velocity Inside Sales Team gives you the knowledge to successfully execute an innovative sales channel strategy."
Dr. Cheemin Bo-Linn, President, Peritus Partners, Former Vice President, IBM

"Being strategic about how to leverage an inside sales channel has never been so critical. This is a timely book. Lori Harmon and Debbi Funk understand how to effectively build high-velocity inside sales teams."
Mark McLaughlin, CEO, Palo Alto Networks

"Lori and Debbi have written a comprehensive guide for building a high-velocity inside sales team. Until now, this information has never been consolidated into a single, easy-to-read handbook. In about an hour you can find out the key elements required and steps to take to build an effective, productive, fired-up inside sales team."
Shelley McNary, Senior Director of Inside Sales, Coveo

"At a time when executives face increased pressure to generate more revenue at a lower cost, Lori Harmon and Debbi Funk show CEOs and sales leaders how to build a cost-effective, highly productive sales model."
Sally Pera, CEO, Association for Corporate Growth, Silicon Valley Chapter

"Companies that excel at growing recurring revenue significantly outperform their competitors. In fact, over the past year, these companies grew revenues 20 percent faster and enjoyed 25 percent higher profit margins than their Fortune 1000 peers. Inside sales is the perfect channel for managing your recurring revenue stream. 42 Rules for Building a High-Velocity Inside Sales Team is the how-to guide for building high performing in-house teams to deliver these outstanding results."
Christine Heckart, EVP, Strategy, Marketing, People & Systems, ServiceSource

"Mentoring and coaching by a front-line manager are critical to the success of your inside sales team! Lori and Debbi describe the importance of this process and other key management aspects of leading a high-velocity inside sales team."
Ingrid B. Steinbergs, Worldwide Vice President, Inside Sales, HPSW, Hewlett-Packard Company

"Inside sales is exploding in growth and the learning curve comes with that. This complex and always changing profession needs direction and that's why 42 Rules for Building a High-Velocity Inside Sales Team is a perfect guide. Lori Harmon and Debbi Funk bring their 40+ years of combined knowledge of leadership and subject-matter expertise in developing this book. You are in good hands with their recommendations and my first rule is to READ IT!!!"
Josiane Chriqui Feigon, President and CEO, TeleSmart Communications

"Having witnessed Lori and Debbi manage their inside sales teams, it's fabulous to see that they have encapsulated their own success factors in such a great and easy 'how-to' book."
Ron Sacchi, Business and Organizational Change Consultant

"42 Rules for Building a High-Velocity Inside Sales Team is one of those rare books that give you actionable strategies, steps, and examples that will help define your approach and, ultimately, the value of your inside sales team. This is a must-read!"
Sally Duby, Vice-President of SMB Sales, Microsoft, Former President Phoneworks

"This easy-to-read book nets out the key factors you need to know for setting up, leading, and optimizing a high-performance inside sales team. Read it and prosper."
Jill Konrath, Author, SNAP Selling, Selling to Big Companies

"42 Rules for Building a High-Velocity Inside Sales Team is a great resource! It's a truly useful book for executives and sales leaders looking to assemble a high-velocity inside sales team. Inside, you'll learn from real-world experiences, what it takes to create a successful inside sales team."
Jill Rowley, Social Selling Evangelist, Oracle

Dedication

For our families who have supported us during the book-writing process, even when it meant sacrificing time with them.

Acknowledgments

Writing a book is both a fun and fulfilling experience. It also happens to be a lot of work! It is not a project that we could have done by ourselves.

Without the mentors that gave us our first opportunity to work in inside sales, this book would never have come about. For Lori, that was Dick Lewis, who believed in her and gave her a number of professional opportunities, including leading her first inside sales team. For Debbi, this was her father, the late Ralph Soden, who supported her leaving the family business to pave her own way as an inside sales professional.

We are fortunate to have worked with so many talented professionals through our careers. It is our network that we leaned upon as we embarked on this journey. A big "thank you" to Shelley McNary and Lisa Sousa, who were our original sounding boards before embarking on this book. It isn't all work!

Along the way we got some much appreciated help from Erin Smith, Lauriel Spooner, Eskander Matta, Joe Fraser, Jenna Green, and Mark Duncan. We can't thank them enough for stepping in when we needed to push through the mental hurdles.

We had some very aggressive deadlines. We relied upon a responsive network to provide us with reviews, feedback, quotes, and endorsements. Many thanks to Dr. Cheemin Bo-Linn, Marina Donovan, Sally Duby, Josiane Feigon, Robert Fioretti, Liz Gelb-O'Connor, Michael Halper, Christine Heckart, Mike LaBelle, Laurie Lacey, Lars Leckie, Jill Konrath, Ken Krogue, Mark McLaughlin, Brian Mory, Sally Pera, Angela Raggio, Jill Rowley, Lori Rush, Ron Sacchi, Ingrid Steinbergs, David Sterenfeld, and John Stringer.

Finally, we want to thank our families, Stephen, Giovanna, Gabriella, Greg, Kevin, and Collin, who encourage and inspire us to push our limits and to try new things, like writing a book!

C o n t e n t s

Foreword by Ken Krogue, Founder and President, InsideSales.com

The pragmatic definition of inside sales is simple: inside sales is remote sales.

It has been called virtual sales, professional sales done remotely, or, one of my favorites, "sales in the cloud." Whereas outside sales are done face-to-face, today most sales are being done remotely.

The term "inside sales" originally came about as an attempt to differentiate "telemarketing" (or "tele-sales") from the more complex, "high-touch," phone-based, business-to-business (B2B), and business-to-consumer (B2C) selling practices.

Telemarketing is believed to have begun in the 1950s. Dial America Marketing is reported to be the first company dedicated to telephone sales and services. By the 1970s, "telemarketing" was a common term used to describe selling over the phone. It often included outbound and inbound sales, but later became more synonymous with calls to lists of names, stereotypically while the family is having dinner.

By the late 1990s, "inside sales" was the term used to differentiate the practice from outside sales—the traditional face-to-face sales model where sales people traveled to the client's location of business.

When I started my first inside sales team in 1991 at Franklin Covey, we were breaking new ground. Outside sales was our primary sales channel.

Since 1991, inside sales has become a mainstream sales channel. In industries like management consulting, advertising/PR, healthcare, and education, it has overtaken outside sales in terms of number of employees.

In 2004, when Dave Elkington and I founded In-sideSales.com, we searched the keyword "inside sales" on Google, and no one else was there. To-day, tens of thousands of companies are trying to hire inside sales reps. What was an experiment has become the fastest growing segment of sales and lead generation.

While inside sales is undeniably effective, it has caused conflicts between younger, disruptive, more technically savvy upstarts selling over the phone, and existing outside sales.

Initially, inside sales was relegated to generating leads for the more senior outside sales reps or merely closing the smaller account. Today, inside sales is a strategic imperative for companies of all sizes, as it has become a high-velocity sales model that quickly delivers significant revenue.

Are you a CEO, CFO, or EVP responsible for sales management? If you are not tracking the trends related to a high-velocity sales model, you run the risk of falling behind your competitors. Don't let that happen. Take an hour to read this book, and share it with friends and colleagues in your profession. Consider how building a high-velocity inside sales team could benefit your organization and keep you ahead of your competitors.

Executive education is critical when building a high-velocity sales team. The rapid growth of inside sales has created a situation where the demand for talent exceeds the supply. Being familiar with the concepts that are covered in this book will help you to find the right talent to lead your high-velocity sales organi-zation and understand whether they are taking the right steps to build and lead the team.

If you are reading this book and are directly in-volved with setting sales strategies and processes within your organization, carve out a small group within your sales organization as your test case. Use this book to educate yourself on the concepts, methods, and processes ascribed to the high-ve-locity sales model, and start applying some or all of the elements of this model to your test team. Compare the results and ROI to your other sales teams to see the benefits of the high-velocity sales model.

There are many sources where one can glean information on how to build a high-velocity inside sales team. Lori Harmon and Debbi Funk have combined their real-life experiences and thought leadership with interviews of other industry experts into a single, easy-to-read book. They have taken a complex process that would take years to learn through experience and reduced it into 42 short, to-the-point rules. These rules give you or your selected inside sales leader a clear path for building a high-velocity inside sales team that will quickly deliver results to your bottom line.

Traditionally, sales has been focused on outside sales reps. These reps had seemingly unlimited expense accounts—they were road warriors traveling over 50 percent of the time to close BIG deals. Sales cycles were long and measurements were quarterly—often resulting in end-of-quarter surprises if a large deal did not close.

Inside sales has broken all of the traditional sales rules.

"Inside sales" originated as a term in the 1980s to differentiate these reps from outside sales reps. Initially, many people were skeptical that it would work. They believed you had to be meeting with a prospect face-to-face, taking them out to play golf, and wining and dining them. In 1995, when I built my first inside sales team, most of my time was spent selling the concept internally and convincing the outside sales team that it would be to their benefit. Outside sales said it would not work. Outside sales was angry because it was eating into their budget. Outside sales was concerned that it would impact their commissions and disenfranchise their customers and prospects.

However, the concept of a lower-cost sales channel was appealing to company executives. Inside sales reps were paid less money, did not need to travel or have big expense accounts. They could contact significantly more prospects and have more prospect meetings on a daily basis. They were measured on weekly and monthly metrics, which improved forecasting accuracy. Fortunately, the executives at the company where I worked were very supportive of building an inside sales team and it paid off as the team grew revenue from $0 to $50 million in two years. According to John Stringer, currently CEO of Producer's Forum and former CEO of Wyse Technology, "Even though I had developed several traditional outside sales forces and, in 1995, was an EVP of Worldwide Sales, I could see early on that inside sales would be a game-changer. With their cost-effective nature and ability to touch so many more customers and prospects on a daily basis, it was clear inside sales would break the rules of traditional sales models."[1]

As the tools evolved and inside sales was given the ability to give presentations, online demos, and then have face-to-face meetings with tools like Skype, there were very few traditional outside sales activities that they could not complete from their desks.

Then, buyers started driving the need for inside sales. Buyers prefer to deal with a person via phone, email, or over the Internet. The process is more efficient for buyers so they are more productive.

A 2009 Market Size Study[2] by Info USA (as cited by Krogue 2013) indicated that inside sales was growing at a rate of 15 times than that of outside sales. With such a large jump in the number of inside sales reps, the BLS.gov & 2013 Market Size Study[3] (also cited by Krogue 2013) from Inside-Sales.com now shows that inside sales is growing three times as fast as outside sales. In 2013, one million inside sales jobs will be added, which is a 26 percent growth rate over 2012.[4] Outside sales reps today spend significantly more time on the phone and are beginning to take on many of the characteristics of inside sales reps. The roles of outside sales and inside sales are coming together but the primary approach is leveraging the phone, Internet, and key productivity tools (Rule 13) to sell.

---

[1] John Stringer (CEO of Producer's Forum), email message to Lori Harmon, July 12, 2013.

[2] Ken Krogue, "The Inside Sales Revolution," *SlideShare*, August 27, 2013, http://www.slideshare.net/insidesales/high-velocity-tour-citrix-ken-small?from_search=1%20(slide%2039).

[3] Ibid.

[4] Bob Perkins, "The Future of Inside Sales" (presentation, Inside Sales Virtual Summit, June 20,2013).

According to Lars Leckie, Managing Partner at venture capital (VC) firm, Hummer Winblad,

> The new high-velocity business model using inside sales is as big of a disrupter to sales as SaaS was to software. This model is a competitive differentiator that will give companies a two-year lead in terms of their growth rate versus the old outside sales model. Venture capitalists will not invest in a company without a well-thought-out inside sales plan. Innovation isn't just for products; companies need innovation in sales too.[5]

---

[5] Lars Leckie, "The High Velocity Business Model" (presentation, Inside Sales Virtual Summit, June 20, 2013), http://vshow.on24.com/vshow/insidesales?l=en#auditorium.

1 Rules Are Meant to Be Broken

The strategic nature of these teams combined with the limited talent available has created a requirement for much more hands-on management.

This book provides you with rules for building a high-velocity inside sales team that are based on our years of experience. They are proven and repeatable. However, it is important to note that every situation is not the same so there needs to be a degree of flexibility.

The concept of inside sales itself was a rule breaker. In more recent years some of the rules about how to hire, structure, and manage an inside sales team have also been broken.

In Rule 8 you will read about hiring. At a time when the job market was highly competitive, it was difficult to find experienced inside sales people. At that time we searched to hire junior reps that had some high technology sales experience and were looking for a career path. The company's internal recruiter was having a hard time sourcing candidates and we had several open positions on the team. It was time to think outside the box. What skills were needed for the position and what could be taught? We hired a candidate with sales experience, but he was in the financial services industry. He was looking to get into high technology and was motivated to learn. If he could successfully sell financial services, then chances are, he could successfully sell other things too. Guess what? He could and he ended up being one of our most successful hires. It is important to note in breaking this rule, extra onboarding and coaching was necessary for him to become successful.

Rule 6 talks about "virtual teams," a concept that used to be taboo. When inside sales teams were started, the best practice was to build centralized teams at your corporate headquarters. Now distributed centralization and virtual teams are common. This is due to the technology now available to enable teams and individuals to work and be managed remotely.

Speaking of technology, inside sales started being completely phone-based. However, email, customer relationship management (CRM) systems, power dialers, web-conferencing technology, and social media have fueled the explosion of the inside sales profession. These services have given these reps numerous ways to find, connect, and communicate with customers and prospects.

The roles of inside sales reps have also broken the original rules. In the beginning, an inside sales rep performed all functions, including lead qualification, closing deals, and managing installed base accounts. Today, these functions have been separated into three individual roles based on the fact that each one requires a different skill set.

Finally, the growth of inside sales has broken the rule of smiling, dialing, and reading scripts. The strategic nature of these teams combined with the limited talent available has created a requirement for much more hands-on management. Coaching and mentoring are more important than ever in building highly motivated, effective, and engaged teams.

While we don't recommend that you intentionally set out to break rules, sometimes you need to be flexible to move forward. The business world is dynamic so very few situations are exactly the same. If you need to break a rule, make sure you have considered the possible outcomes.

What rules have you broken with a positive outcome?

Section I
Strategy, Planning, and Alignment

You are considering building an inside sales team. Great! Before you start hiring, consider your goals and objectives to effectively plan out your inside sales strategy. Know what kind(s) of inside sales team(s) you plan to build and the profile of the candidates that will be hired.

2 Have a Go-to-Market Strategy

We...proved that [inside sales] could win a high close rate at one-third the cost and in one-third the time.

Let's face the facts; your product and/or service address a unique market segment. You need to take a close look at what defines your target market and what value you bring to it before determining if building an inside sales team is right for your company. It is critical that every company has a go-to-market strategy.

Start with a clear understanding of the following:

- What products are you selling? One or many?
- Who is your customer/prospect—are your sales business-to-business (B2B) or business-to-consumer (B2C)?
- Who is your competition?
- What is their "go-to-market" strategy?
- What is *their* competitive advantage?
- What is *your* competitive advantage?

Once you answer these questions you can begin to design a sales strategy, position your company to go to market, and win the game.

Now let's break it down by buyer type—consumer or business?

If your product is targeted at the consumer (B2C), then you must consider the profile of your most likely buyer.

- Gender
- Age
- Demographic
- What value does your product provide?
- Where do they shop (retail, high-end department store, online, discount stores)?
- What is your distribution method (direct sales, retail sales, channel distribution)?

If you are targeting a business (B2B) as your buyer, then the following needs to be determined.

- What type of companies will purchase your products(large enterprises, small to medium businesses, Original Equipment Manufacturers (OEMs), Value Added Resellers (VARs), Systems Integrators (SIs), resellers, distributors, or a combination of all of these?
- What market verticals are you targeting?
- What titles in the target companies will make the purchase decision? Will these titles be reachable via telephone? For example, doctors are rarely available by phone and require a face-to-face sales approach, whereas real estate agents are easy to reach; corporate contacts are somewhere in between.
- What are your price points?
- What is your (estimated) average deal size?
- What is your (estimated) length-of-sales cycle?
- How will you sell it? This is where your channel strategy comes in.

Armed with this information you will be able to determine if it makes sense for your company to build an inside sales team. Inside sales teams are typically used in the following situations:

- To uncover and qualify leads for outside sales, an inside sales team that closes business, or recruits and manages channel partners
- To close deals over the phone (typically up to $50,000 but this is not a hard and fast rule) with direct customers or through channel partners.
- To team with an outside sales team to advance larger deals (greater than $50,000) through the sales cycle.

A great example of a company using their go-to-market strategy to begin sales with an inside sales team is Salesforce.com. When the company started they were selling their SaaS customer relationship management (CRM) solution to small and medium businesses. The price point and target market did not support having an outside sales team. According to Marc Benioff in his book *Behind the Cloud*, "We ... proved that [inside sales] could win a high close rate at one-third the cost and in one-third the time as the traditional selling model."[6]

Only when Salesforce.com added enterprise accounts to their target market did they begin investing in an outside sales force.

As a rule, any organization can benefit from the economics of an inside sales organization. The lower the average deal size and the shorter the sales cycle, the more it makes sense to utilize an inside sales team.

What is your go-to-market strategy?

---

[6] Marc Benioff and Carlyle Adler, *Behind the Cloud: The Untold Story of How Salesforce.com Went from Idea to Billion-Dollar Company—and Revolutionized an Industry* (San Francisco: Jossey-Bass, 2009).

3 Understand the Funnel

The sales funnel is a simple, visual representation of the sales process.

For those that have never been in sales, your sales funnel is a key component of building your high-velocity inside sales team.

The sales funnel is a simple, visual representation of the sales process. The top is wide and it is where all of the inquiries flow into the funnel. The middle is where your qualification takes place, and the bottom is your closed business being converted into revenue.

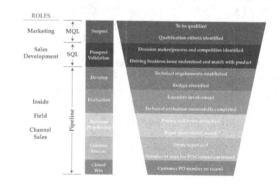

This traditional representation was meant to illustrate a simple breakdown of sales stages, number and value of each opportunity in the funnel, and the conversion rate between each sales stage. As technology, business models, and communication preferences have changed, the funnel has become more complicated. Leads and opportunities now flow in and out of the funnel at different stages of the process.

At the very top of the funnel, inquiries from potential buyers come in. These are then nurtured by marketing until they become marketing qualified leads (MQLs). MQLs are passed to sales development for live qualification. If they meet the qualification criteria they become sales qualified leads (SQLs). SQLs get converted to opportunities and these move through the remainder of the sales stages.

Once an SQL is converted to an opportunity it becomes part of the sales pipeline. The sales pipeline is the set of opportunities that have a potential to close at a specified date. The total number of opportunities in the pipeline with a close date of the current quarter is called the "current quarter pipeline." The set of deals with close dates during future quarters is the "future quarter pipeline." The combination of the current quarter and future quarter pipeline deals is considered "all pipeline."

The design of the sales funnel is to provide sales reps and sales management with a visual of the company's sales process. It also helps to identify trends and performance associated with a lead going through the funnel and becoming a closed deal; in other words, going through the pipeline.

A basic sales funnel will show sales management a picture of the pipeline opportunities broken down by sales stage (Rule 25). Sales management can see how many opportunities their team is working on and what stages most opportunities are in.

Looking at a sales funnel over time will allow you to see if the number of opportunities are growing or shrinking. Measuring conversion rates between each stage of the funnel and between MQLs, SQLs, and closed deals will provide valuable metrics for forecasting and budgeting for pipeline development requirements.

The sales funnel allows sales management to measure deal velocity, or how long an opportunity is in each sales stage. Knowing where opportunities get slowed down is an area where improvements can be made to accelerate your entire sales process.

At one company, we determined that Sales Stage 2 and Sales Stage 5 were the stages that took the longest in the sales process. Sales Stage 2 was where success criteria for the deal were established. Sales Stage 5 was the process where the contract was negotiated. Since the longer of those two was the contracting process we decided to tackle that one first to shorten the overall sales cycle. We made a number of improvements in both automation and the approval process involving finance and legal. The end result was a 52 percent improvement in Stage 5 and a 20 percent improvement in the entire sales process, taking the average sales cycle from eight months to six months.

What does your sales funnel look like?

4 Know What Type of Team You Need

Over the years inside sales has become more specialized.

When inside sales teams were first started, the inside sales reps would perform all of the different selling tasks: lead identification and qualification, selling new business and managing installed base accounts. Over the years inside sales has become more specialized based on their targeted results and the different skills required to perform the various functions.

This rule defines the different types of inside sales teams that you should consider when implementing a high-velocity inside sales channel.

- **Sales or Business Development:** in a direct sales environment, the purpose of a sales development team is to increase revenue by identifying and generating qualified leads that increase the number of opportunities in the pipeline. These reps uncover qualified leads either by following up on or nurturing marketing qualified leads (MQLs), leveraging social selling skills or cold calling. Once they identify a sales qualified lead (SQL), the sales development rep (SDR) sets a meeting with the qualified lead and the appropriate sales rep. SDRs do not close business.

- **Channel Sales Development:** SDRs working primarily with channel partners have the same purpose as SDRs in a direct sales environment. However, their responsibility is to indirectly increase revenue through channel partners. Their activities may be expanded beyond those described above for direct sales SDRs. SDRs supporting a channel sales model can be assigned to perform channel-specific campaigns. These campaigns help onboard and ramp up a channel partner faster with the goal of helping the partners become self-sufficient and able to close deals on their own. Examples include: calling campaigns to the partner's installed base or lead list to generate interest in new products, hosting on-site partner visits so the partner can listen to the SDR calls, and/or help fill seats at a partner event.

- **Inside Sales:** the purpose of inside sales is to remotely generate revenue for the company by closing deals. These teams can be structured in several different ways.

  - If a company has deals with short sales cycles and low dollar values that can be closed in one to two calls, MQLs can be passed directly to inside sales and closed. There is no need for an SDR team.
  - For longer sales cycles, inside sales would receive SQLs from SDRs. Depending on the deal size (Rule 2) and buyer buying preferences, inside sales reps can then manage the lead through the entire sales cycle and close the business. They may also be partnered with outside sales reps and jointly manage the lead through the sales cycle (Rule 20).
  - Inside sales reps can be focused only on managing installed base accounts. This would include selling additional products to installed base accounts and/or renewing installed base contracts.
  - Renewal sales can be separated into a renewals inside sales team (Rule 27).
  - When channel partners are involved, inside sales can manage prospects through the sales cycle and then pass the deal to a channel partner for fulfillment. Channel inside sales make up 17 percent of the inside sales models in today's market.[7]

- **Lead Researcher[8] or Sales Enablement Reps:** a new inside sales role that is in its infancy is a lead researcher or sales enablement rep. These reps clean and enhance the lead data with contact phone numbers and company information, such as company size, number of employees, and other profile information. They may also clean up installed base information and create quotes for renewal customers. This offloads a lot of the administrative work from the SDRs and inside sales reps so that they can quickly contact the lead or installed base customer and advance them through the sales cycle.

What type(s) of inside sales team(s) will you build?

---

[7] Bob Perkins, "The Future of Inside Sales."
[8] Ken Krogue, "The Inside Sales Revolution."

5 Don't Be Afraid to Ask for Expert Advice

Founders are engineers. Sales, particularly inside sales, is their blind spot. So, they need to get educated.

The rapid growth of inside sales has created a talent gap. There is more demand for experienced talent than available talent with experience. One of the reasons for writing this book is to help CEOs, Vice Presidents of Sales, and new sales managers who don't have the knowledge and experience with inside sales to understand how to build a team or what to look for when hiring someone to build a team.

For companies building new teams, it is imperative to get some help and find people that have done it before. Because building and leading inside sales is a specialized skill set, you want a person who has built a team previously. This will save your company time and money, getting the model started with a best practice approach. If you can hire a leader with experience in building a high-velocity inside sales team, do so. Otherwise, bring in a consulting firm that specializes in inside sales to build the team for you. Then, either during the process or once the team is built, the consulting firm can train and mentor the person who has been selected to lead the team.

This challenge is especially true for start-up companies. Lars Leckie of Hummer Winblad states, "Founders are engineers. Sales, particularly inside sales, is their blind spot. So, they need to get educated."[9] In fact, this is so important for start-up

---

[9] Lars Leckie, "The High Velocity Business Model."

companies that venture capital firms, like True Ventures and Andreessen Horowitz, have added advisors or partners specifically to help their portfolio companies build high-velocity inside sales teams.

This is the approach I used to build my first inside sales team. The company I worked for was debating whether they should build an inside sales team orinvest more in outside sales. At that point I was the Director of Professional Services with no prior experience with inside sales. At that time, few people in the industry understood what inside sales was and how it should operate. We brought in an outside consulting firm to help us develop the business case and teach me how to build and run an inside sales team. That foundation led to numerous professional opportunities to build, lead, and turn around inside sales organizations. Without the help of the consulting firm, the speed with which we were able to execute and deliver results would not have been as favorable: the team grew from $0 to $50 million dollars in two years.

It can be hard to admit that you need to engage someone with a specialized background to assist with your efforts. It should be considered, however, if you do not have an inside sales background. Even if you have an outside sales background, realize that inside sales is a different discipline. The upfront investment will help insure your success.

The industry is changing rapidly. To be effective, leaders need to stay current with the trends in inside sales.

In addition to consulting firms, the American Association of Inside Sales Professionals (AA-ISP), LinkedIn groups like Inside Sales Experts and Inside Sales Managers, and blogs (Appendix A) can help a person stay current with the latest developments in the inside sales arena.

Where will you go to find help when you need it?

6 Choose Your Location

This all depends on the culture of the company and the strength of the sales leadership.

In the 1980s, best practice was having a centralized inside sales team that could be effectively managed. Technology was less sophisticated than it is today. The centralized model allowed for economies of scale with costs related to computer and telephone technologies.

In the 1990s, the technology to support decentralized teams was still not available. At that time I worked for a company that had disbanded their centralized inside sales team and placed "telesales" reps (managed by the outside sales managers) in the field offices with the outside sales reps. Instead of spending time on the phone uncovering leads they were tasked with delivering demo equipment to prospect locations, completing paperwork for the outside sales reps, and getting coffee and lunch for the office. Outside sales reps and management complained that they did not have enough leads. This was obviously because there was no discipline around making proactive outbound calls to uncover leads.

Today, there are three primary organizational structures for an inside sales team:

- Centralized
- Decentralized
- Virtual

Centralized

This has been the most common way to structure an inside sales team. Reasons for centralizing an inside sales team are:

- Easier to manage workers and create an energy that improves morale

- Effective coaching and mentoring through face-to-face interactions
- Better communications and the ability to have impromptu meetings
- Minimal distractions
- Consistent training
- Flexibility for some workers to work early shifts that may be desired for family schedules

Decentralized

Above a certain size (at least 10 reps), some companies implement decentralized centralization. This means having several "at scale" teams in different locations. This enables companies headquartered in expensive geographic locations to reduce costs and pull from a broader talent pool.

Virtual

The advent of SaaS-based CRM systems, VoIP phones, and tools like Skype, GoToMeeting, and WebEx has made virtual teams possible. Previously, there was no way for a manager to monitor the key activity metrics for remote reps. Today, with consistent rep usage of these tools and management oversight, inside sales management has the ability to track rep activities, such as listening to calls, coaching, and managing reps nearly as effectively as if they were all in a centralized location. Additionally, virtual teams require strong management leadership and experienced sales reps that are excellent communicators and have a proven track record.

Reasons for implementing a virtual team include:

- Access to a broader talent pool
- Potential reduction of cost for office space and personnel
- Geographically matched time zone support
- Ability to offer a career path to an outside sales role

Angela Raggio managed inside sales teams at a Fortune 500 company for 11 years. She preferred managing virtual teams as it "provides a flexible work environment and empowers them [the reps] to be independent in achieving their goals."[10]

A recent survey by Scott Edinger reported that team members who work remotely were more engaged and committed than people working in the office.[11]

Team morale can be high in any of the above models. This all depends on the culture of the company and strength of the sales leadership.

What location(s) will you select for your inside sales team(s)?

[10] Angela Raggio in discussion with Debbi Funk, September 4, 2013.
[11] Scott Edinger, "Why Remote Workers Are More (Yes, More), Engaged," *Harvard Business Review* (blog), August 24, 2012 (8:00 a.m.), http://blogs.hbr.org/cs/2012/08/are_you_taking_your_people_for.html.

7 Inside Sales Should Report into Sales

A recent study from the Bridge Group found that 70 percent of inside sales teams report into sales.

When companies are small, individuals often take on multiple roles. With resource constraints, companies simply need to get the job done. When this happens, inside sales can be built and managed by a group other than sales.

For example, marketing may be frustrated that they are generating leads that are not being followed up on or being cherry picked by sales. To fix the problem, marketing starts a sales development team. Frequently, they lack the knowledge and experience to hire reps with the right sales skills. How can they interview for sales skills when they are not sales people themselves? They also are not familiar with the processes, metrics, and training required to ensure the success of a sales development team. Finally, the sales development team may not be aligned with sales.

According to a study by the Bridge Group, Inc., marketing is less experienced at ramping a team that has to have conversations with buyers. They don't have the process, methodologies, and tools in place that will shorten the time to productivity. They found that inbound-focused teams that report to marketing have an average 4.5 month ramp, while those reporting to sales ramp in just three months.[12]

When reporting to marketing, sales development is often tasked with activities that are better served by other more administrative personnel,

---

[12] Ibid.

like cleaning up the CRM database, creating manual reports, or attending broader marketing meetings. These activities take sales development off the phone and away from their primary task of uncovering qualified leads.

During a company-wide reorganization, the sales development team I was managing under the sales organization was realigned to report into the marketing department. As a sales development team, we had always worked closely with both sales and marketing, and goals were aligned, so the change seemed minimal at first.

The metrics analyzed by marketing are very different from those that drive the sales team. As an example, marketing wants to know how many of the leads they have generated have been contacted while not considering the prioritization of the prospect profile. Sales is focused on how many leads become pipeline opportunities. The day-to-day activities of the team became more focused on the ROI and data around marketing campaigns than delivering leads that would create revenue opportunities for sales. Lead quality and quantity passed to the sales team started to decline. The outside sales team began complaining as their pipelines were being negatively impacted.

Our experience is that inside sales should report into the sales organization. A recent study from the Bridge Group found that 70 percent of inside sales teams report into sales.[13]

Because inside sales is a specialty area within the broader sales organization, the team requires specific management skills. When an outside sales leader is tasked with managing an inside sales team, there can be a lack of understanding of the required tools, metrics, and processes required for inside sales. In this structure, inside sales can end up becoming an extension or administrative support to outside sales.

Having inside sales report to a knowledgeable inside sales leader as part of the broader sales organization will enable them to be aligned with the broader sales team (if there is one); utilize the right systems, tools, processes, and metrics; and be effectively motivated.

Where will your inside sales team(s) report?

---

[13] Ibid.

8 Define Your Ideal Inside Sales Rep Qualifications

Before hiring any inside sales reps, you need to define the skills and qualifications required to be successful for each position.

Before hiring any inside sales reps, you need to define the skills and qualifications required to be successful for each position.

When building a new team, it is best to hire reps with prior experience in sales development or inside sales, depending on which type of team you are assembling. Experienced reps will ramp up faster and have higher productivity than reps without prior relevant experience. In order for the team to be successful as a whole and prove themselves as a valuable asset to the company they will have to deliver results quickly.

Here's a typical profile for a sales development rep:

- Minimum one to two years successful experience in sales development in a similar technology environment
- Proven track record achieving measurable lead development goals in a highly automated sales environment
- Experience with using social media and cold calling
- BS/BA degree or equivalent from an accredited college or university

For inside sales reps there are more variables, depending on how the position is structured. Typical experienced inside sales rep requirements are:

- Minimum three to five years successful experience in inside sales in a similar technology and distribution channel environment

- Similar experience in a similar type of sales environment (new business, account management, or renewals)
- Proven track record achieving measurable sales goals in a highly automated sales environment
- Experience with using social media and cold calling
- BS/BA degree or equivalent from an accredited college or university

The initial review of potential candidates for both the sales development role and the inside sales role should include screening for the following skills:

- Voicemail messaging—etiquette and effectiveness
- Email (written) communication skills—etiquette and effectiveness
- Follow-up skills
- Effective phone presence (tone, pace, volume)
- Qualification of the position/opportunity
- Process understanding

For the new inside sales role outlined in Rule 4, the lead researcher, or sales enablement position, the requirements would be:

- Minimum two to five years administration experience, preferably in sales processes
- Ability to interpret raw data and conduct basic analysis
- Ability to research data utilizing different databases
- Ability to manage specific tasks through prescribed processes and use critical thinking to bridge process gaps on non-standard tasks
- Demonstrated ability to communicate quickly and succinctly in CRM workflow, email, and by voice
- Ability to manage, prioritize, and communicate about competing deadlines
- College degree preferred

These skills are non-negotiable. You can validate them through role-play scenarios with the candidates during the hiring process. Note subjective cues during your interviews. Are they a team player? Do they have the right degree of motivation?

There will be other elements to your job description that will help you to recruit the right candidates. However, it is not very often that you will meet a candidate that meets all of your criteria. You need to be clear on what are core to the success in the role. The rest can be prioritized.

If you already have an established inside sales team in place, recent college graduates or "hungry," less experienced candidates (coming from outside of technology, call center, or corporate environments) can be viable candidates. A side benefit to using less experienced reps is that peer reps can act as mentors.

What are the qualifications required for the candidates on your inside sales team(s)?

9 Define a Qualified Lead

Defining a qualified lead is a key foundation in any successful inside sales organization.

The term "lead" is often loosely used in an organization. Different departments and personnel have varying definitions. Ensuring a consistent cross-functional definition of all the different interpretations of a lead is critical.

Below are definitions of the most common types of leads:

- **Raw leads:** contacts coming from purchased lists or lists brought to a company by a new sales rep. No marketing activity has occurred against these leads. They include: company, contact name, phone number, and/or email address.

- **Inquiry:** contacts in a company's target market that have responded to a marketing campaign. They require further nurturing by the marketing department and may or may not have the title of the decision maker. They include: company, contact name, phone number, and/or email address.

- **Lead:** contacts in a company's target market. They have the target title or higher and have requested information from the company. They require follow-up from a sales development rep. These include: company, contact name, phone number, and/or email address.

- **Qualified lead:** a lead with whom a rep has had a conversation and confirmed that the contact meets the criteria for a qualified lead (see below) and they have agreed to meet with a sales person. Based on their level of quality, these leads are typically rated A or B (Rule 11).

- **Disqualified lead:** a lead with whom a rep has engaged in conversation and has determined that the prospect does not fit the criteria to become a qualified lead.

Note: with the exception of raw leads, all of the lead types above should be captured in the company's CRM system.

Qualified leads feed your sales teams regardless of whether they are outside or inside sales (Rule 18). A key foundation in any successful inside sales organization is establishing and communicating your company's definition of a qualified lead and the qualification with subsequent follow-up process.

I worked with a software company that was having problems generating enough leads for their sales teams. The sales development team was passing only a single qualified lead per rep per week and felt like failures for starving the sales team. The inside and outside sales teams that were supposed to be receiving the leads were missing their quotas. No one was happy.

What was the problem? The definition of a qualified lead was too stringent. It required the sales development team to get the lead to the point where it was an opportunity nearly ready to close. It was preventing the true "sales" teams from doing what they do best—sell! The company was missing out on opportunities because the sales development reps did not have the bandwidth to contact more prospects.

Initially, a qualified lead had to meet the following criteria:

- Decision makers, process, timeframe (<12 months) identified
- Problem or pain was identified and could be resolved by the company's product
- Budget was identified
- Competition identified
- Technical requirements established
- Active project had been launched

We changed the definition of a qualified lead or meeting to be "a prospect in an account targeted by your company." The contact had to have:

- Authority in the decision process
- Problem or pain and a desire to solve it that can be resolved by the product the company is offering
- Sense of urgency to solve the problem within the next 12 months
- Budget or access to budget to solve the problem

By simply changing the definition, the number of qualified leads passed to sales increased by 150 percent. You always have to be willing to make adjustments, as you will read about again in Rule 41.

What is your definition of a qualified lead?

10 Allocate Resources to Qualify Inbound Leads

Inbound leads are 61 percent less expensive than outbound leads. Timely contact can maximize lead conversion rates.

When analyzing your optimum inside sales structure, you must be clear about your objectives. Of course, the end result is always "increased sales." The key question to ask is, "How are we going to get there?" It sounds simple and basic, yet it is a huge decision that should be based upon where you have gaps in meeting your revenue objectives. You likely have a sales team of some kind in place. Where can an inside sales team augment and enhance their efforts in driving revenue?

Inbound leads are 61 percent less expensive than outbound leads.[14] Timely contact can maximize lead conversion rates (Rule 34). Therefore, you want to make sure sufficient resources are available to process the inbound leads in the optimal timeframe. One way to determine the number of hires you should have initially would be to figure out your approximate MQL volume and then work from there.

To determine the number of required MQLs, start with the company's revenue goals. Divide that number by your average deal size. If you are not certain about your average deal size, use an estimate so you can put a stake in the ground.

*Total Revenue / Average Deal Size
= Number of Deals required to achieve your Revenue objective*

How many deals do you have to have in your pipeline to close a single deal? Again, if you are a new company this will not be a known metric. So, you

---

[14] Ibid.

can estimate that for every five opportunities, you will realize one deal. This can be verified after you begin to measure the true conversion rate.

Number of Deals x 5 = Number of opportunities required

How many leads does it take to create a single opportunity? This will vary by company, industry, and marketing campaign effectiveness. For the purposes of this example, we will use 10 MQLs for one opportunity.

Number of opportunities x 10 = Number of leads required

There is no set number of leads that marketing should generate for sales. Of course, sales is always going to say "the more the better." Recent changes in buyer behavior and social media will force more leads to come through marketing. Again, for our model, let's assume 40 percent of the leads come from marketing.

Number of required leads x .4 = Number of MQLs

To determine the number of reps required to provide adequate follow-up on these leads, assume a well-known metric for a B2B sales model of 50 calls/emails per day (without a predictive dialer). The formula is:

50 calls/emails x 22 days = 1,100 call/emails per month per rep

Most MQLs require multiple call attempts. You can't assume that making 1,100 calls/month is equivalent to processing 1,100 MQLs/month. For B2B sales, the average connect rate is somewhere between 10 to 20 percent. Assuming a 20 percent contact rate, your rep will only be connecting with 10 of those potential prospects each day.

In Rule 34 (on optimizing lead conversion) we state that six calls and six emails are optimal for inbound leads, although some will be contacted on the first attempt. Multiple attempts must be factored into the productivity metrics. To determine the true number of individual MQLs that can be contacted by each rep takes monitoring and refinement of the model. For the sake of starting out, use the following assumptive formula:

Number of MQLs per month/407 (number of unique MQL attempts per month by rep) = Number of reps required

(This number is based on our collective experience.)

If your sales development team has a blended role, with MQL follow-up and outbound prospecting, then you will need to adjust the metrics accordingly. Outbound prospecting takes time to research and to identify the decision maker, so it will reduce the number of call and email attempts metrics. Because the conversion rate for cold calls is lower, there will also be fewer pipeline opportunities generated.

How many sales development reps will you hire?

11 Establish Lead Scoring Definitions

*Time is money.
It's critical to
prioritize inside
sales team efforts
so they are spent
wisely.*

Time is money. It's critical to prioritize inside sales team efforts so they are spent wisely. The lead follow-up process must be designed and agreed upon by both sales and marketing leaders. You must decide which leads will become MQLs for sales development or inside sales follow-up, and which leads will be nurtured until they meet MQL criteria.

According to Marketo in "The Big List of Lead Scoring Rules,"

> Lead scoring is a shared sales and marketing methodology for ranking leads in order to determine their sales-readiness. Leads are scored based on the interest they show in your business, place in the buying cycle, and their fit with regard to your business.

There are various ways a company can score leads. Either by assigning points, implementing rankings like A, B, C, or D or using terms like "hot," "warm," or "cold." The key point is that by clarifying what exactly constitutes a sales-ready lead, marketing and sales can increase efficiency and productivity.[15]

Here is a simple example where the rating is assigned by the marketing automation system and is based strictly by active project and timeframe (Marketo offers 50+ explicit scores to consider):

---

[15] Marketo, "The Big List of Lead Scoring Rules: A Checklist of Over 250 Explicit and Implicit Lead Scoring Rules," *Marketo*, 2011, http://www.marketo.com/_assets/uploads/Marketo-Lead-Scoring.pdf.

Active Project	Timeframe	Score
Yes	Immediately or 3-6 months	A
(blank)/No	Immediately or 3-6 months	B
Yes	7-12 months	B
(blank)/No	7-12 months or Over 12 months	C
Yes	Over 12 months, Unknown or (blank)	C
(blank)/No	Unknown or (blank)	D
No	Unknown	X

A, B, and maybe C would be routed in the CRM for follow-up, while D and X will not. It is far more efficient to do this initially, then to later waste inside sales' time scrubbing data.

Why is this so important? Suppose your company hosted a webinar with overwhelming attendance. With a large one-time volume of leads, your sales development team doesn't have the bandwidth for timely follow-up. Your lead scoring system can identify people who attended for informational purposes or do not resemble your buyer profile. With correct lead ratings, SDRs can first follow up with the A-rated MQLs first. They avoid wasting time with leads that have incomplete contact information.

Taking it a step further, some leads have a higher conversion rate than others—not all A and B rated leads are equal. You can address this by having your inside team assign priorities as they go through their leads. For example, anyone visiting your website and requesting information (this also goes for email) should be top priority. Next are informational marketing mechanisms, such as white paper downloads and webinars, with a priority given to actual attendees. Lastly are trade show or conference show names. I use names because this has been what is traditionally collected. Trade shows are more of a numbers game where the conversion rate tends to be relatively low.

Automated lead scores are not always correct but should be refined along the way with continuous feedback between the inside sales and the marketing teams. This will help you to avoid an issue that I have seen in the past where the sales team has a perception that the marketing leads "stink."

What are your lead rating definitions?

Section II
Getting Started

By now, you have an understanding of what type of inside sales team(s) will be best for your organization. Now it is time to start building your team and, in parallel, implementing the necessary infrastructure for a successful operation.

12

Hire a Qualified Leader

Inside sales is a unique discipline. It is a different way of selling from the days of the door-to-door salesman. It requires a leader or manager that fully embraces the inside sales discipline with several years of experience in leading successful inside sales teams.

This person should understand how to motivate a team, the key productivity tools and metrics required, and how to properly structure an incentive program for inside sales. He or she should be able to clearly articulate the value of inside sales, work collaboratively with other functional areas, and effectively communicate at all levels of an organization, both internally and externally. Since the inside sales leader will be building a team, it is preferable that he or she have prior experience in building teams from the ground up, or you should plan to leverage external experts (Rule 5) to get them started.

Early in my career, outside sales was the 800-pound gorilla in the sales organization. Generally, the Vice President of Sales had been a career outside sales professional. Therefore, all sales considerations and any rules of engagement were biased toward the outside sales team. Today, it is common to find a sales vice president with some of their individual background in inside sales.

It is critical that the inside sales leader has a clear understanding of the goals, metrics, and skills needed to be successful in the capacity they are managing. If you are considering appointing a manager from internal talent, here are some important considerations:

- Not all good sales people make good managers
- There are challenges promoting from within

While not all sales people make good managers, this is a general statement. When promoting from within, be sure your manager has skills other than being a top sales person. He or she needs to have leadership and solid interpersonal skills.

When promoting from within, ensure that your new manager will be someone who can gain the respect of the new team. Ideally, the person promoted will have already proven him or herself as a figurative leader. This will be especially helpful if they will be managing any of their peers. You will also need to allow for a transition period and set executive expectations accordingly.

The overall objective of the inside sales team leader is to drive the team to meet and exceed their quota, whether this is based on qualified leads, pipeline contribution, revenue, or other metrics. The inside sales team leader is responsible for hiring, training, and motivating their team. This includes regular call monitoring, one-on-one coaching, and weekly forecast reviews. He or she is responsible for defining and implementing the ongoing training that is geared to inside sales (Rule 38) and ensuring the necessary productivity tools are in place (Rule 13). The leader has to be familiar with the required metrics, and implement and monitor them to understand whether individual production standards are being met. Leveraging activity metrics will help your inside sales team leader to understand why the team is not achieving their qualified lead or revenue goals (if that is the case).

The inside sales team leader's collaboration with other departments (like marketing) is imperative to ensuring the team is fed MQLs and has the proper sales enablement tools to be successful. Conducting regular calls with outside sales to validate lead quality and territory coverage is another key touchpoint. To keep the organization "best of class" they have to stay abreast of new inside sales technologies and trends.

The optimal reporting structure for an inside sales manager is eight reps per manager.[16] Higher ratios prevent the manager from performing key functions. The functions that typically slip when the ratio is too high are coaching and mentoring individual reps and coordinating ongoing training. These are key foundational management activities for inside sales leaders and for their reps to be successful.

Who will lead your inside sales team to success?

---

[16] Scott Gruher, "The Optimal Sales Manager to Rep Ratio," *Sales & Marketing Effectiveness* (Sales Benchmark Index blog), May 4, 2011, http://www.salesbenchmarkindex. com/bid/49276/The-Optimal-Sales-Manager-to-Rep-Ratio.

13 Invest in Sales 2.0 Productivity Tools

Creating a scalable, predictable, high-velocity inside sales "machine" requires investing in productivity tools.

Creating a scalable, predictable, high-velocity inside sales "machine" requires investing in productivity tools. Inside sales lowers your cost of sale because of these tools. Every hour lost to non-selling tasks translates into a 14 percent loss in sales productivity.[17]

The minimum set of required tools is a computer; telephone with hands-free headset; Internet connection; email; customer relationship management (CRM) system; and social media accounts, such as LinkedIn or Facebook (Rule 23).

In an office, your phone system should provide you with metrics reports (dials, connects, talk time). For virtual inside sales reps, a VoIP telephone is required to collect the required information to manage individuals remotely.

While many small companies think that they can use an Excel spreadsheet to track metrics, leads, and opportunities, this is not advised. Over time, the data becomes disorganized and time-consuming to sort through. There are many CRM tools available to meet the needs of any sized company. SaaS-based tools are the most popular because they are quick to deploy and easy to customize to your company's unique sales process. A CRM tool allows reps to track and manage a prospect from the time it is a lead through the sales process to being a closed opportunity. They can record com-

---

[17] "AA-ISP Service Provider Directory," *American Association of Inside Sales Professionals*, August 24, 2013, http://www.aa-isp.org/serviceDirectory.php?url=category5.

pleted activities and set future tasks required to manage a sales cycle, understand their pipeline, forecast revenue, and track wins and losses. The CRM provides management with reports required to understand whether a rep has the right activity level, what is working, and what is not during a sales process.

For high-volume call requirements, consider a power dialer. Power dialers provide one-click dialing, voice messaging, email, inbound availability, call recording, and local presence, enabling reps to connect with leads and prospects faster and more consistently. Power dialers can increase call volumes by up to eight times,[18] determine optimal call times, and record the necessary call metrics in the CRM system. Their call recording capability allows management to coach and mentor reps after a call is completed.

Before a lead is loaded into the CRM system, a best-practice approach is to have inquiries processed, nurtured, and scored within a marketing automation system. Using these systems, companies can manage their direct mail campaigns, adhere to anti-spam rules, implement lead nurturing programs, and rank leads based on prospect behavior prior to sending them to sales. Leads loaded into the CRM from a marketing automation solution are considered MQLs. These are the only leads that should be passed to sales, preferably to a sales development team, for further qualification before being sent to a sales rep.

Sales intelligence tools are often needed to enable pre-call research so reps can find out specific information about a company to help personalize their calling efforts. There are vast numbers of these tools available and many of these are integrated within CRM tools. Information about the specific contact can be gleaned from social media resources as discussed in Rule 23.

To perform customer demos and/or give presentations, the team needs a screen-sharing or webcasting application.

For some helpful information on the tools mentioned in this rule, use this website as a reference - http://www.smartsellingtools.com/2013-top-sales-tools.

The key to success with productivity tools is monitoring and enforcing their usage. In a best-practices scenario a productivity tool audit would be performed with results and actions presented quarterly. No processes or reporting requirements should be requested outside what can be provided by the productivity tools that have been implemented. Manual processes undermine the tools usage and impact timely, accurate results reporting.

What productivity tools will your inside sale(s) team need?

---

[18] "Inside Sales Dialer," *InsideSales.com*, August 24, 2013, http://www.insidesales.com/outbound_power_dialer.php.

Develop an Onboarding Process

Without an onboarding program, your new reps cannot reach their full potential and the potential for turnover is greatly increased.

To get reps started properly and minimize their ramp-up period, they should be introduced to the organization through a thorough onboarding program. Without an onboarding program, your new reps cannot reach their full potential and the potential for turnover is greatly increased. Onboarding is a training process for new hires that introduces them to the company, facility, buyer profiles, solutions, job responsibilities, compensation, metrics and measurements, sales processes, and sales tools they need to know to be successful in their new position and get up to speed quickly.

After spending the time and money to hire top talent, you can't afford to neglect having an onboarding process. This is why this program should be developed before a new hire begins their first day. Ad hoc training takes far longer than necessary to get a new hire trained and up to speed. Also, the program is part of a new hire's first-day experience. This experience is key to employee engagement as it establishes the relationship foundation between the company and the employee.

Imagine a new sales rep coming to work on their first day and no one seems to know they are starting. When they finally are shown to their cube, it is full of items left by the previous person who sat at that desk. The new sales rep does not have a computer or a phone, doesn't know where to get coffee, or where the bathrooms are. How do you think that employee is going to feel about your company?

The effort of new-hire training is a cross-functional one, requiring contributions from multiple departments to cover the required content.

At the end of the day, the frontline manager should be sure to check in to answer any questions, fill in any gaps that may occur, and get feedback on the process.

Of course, this does not mean that the onboarding process ends after just a few days. New sales reps do not need to know everything after one week. Set realistic timeframes on when expectations have to be met. For example, after two weeks, the new rep should be able to effectively articulate the company's value proposition.

The sales manager should be observing the new hire as they begin to engage with customers and buyers, listening to calls, reviewing sample voicemails and emails, and coaching the rep to help him or her improve. In order to check skills development and improvement along the way, the sales manager should also have the rep perform written exams, and simulated sales calls and group presentations. Once the rep has sufficient knowledge, he or she should develop a territory plan to demonstrate the steps it will take to deliver the required results. This is also a good time for the sales rep to create an individual development plan to focus on the skills he or she wants to develop the most.

Delivering onboarding with a centralized team can all be completed at a single location. When you are responsible for decentralized teams or virtual teams, having the technology to enable effective delivery is key. This can include combining on-site visits with video conferencing and/or screen-sharing technology.

A sample agenda for onboarding is included in Appendix B.

What is your plan to address new hire onboarding?

15 Set and Monitor Metrics

Tracking metrics is the fastest way to get to a scalable, repeatable sales model.

Metrics are essential for management to understand if reps are on track to deliver results and identify areas for improvement. Metrics are necessary for making continuous improvements and refinements and need to be actionable and predictable. While there are many standard metrics, many will be unique to your sales environment. It is important to select and track only the metrics critical to your operation and that incent the behavior you want from your sales organization. Too many metrics can overwhelm your team. See our list of metrics in Appendix C.

Ideally, you want to start tracking metrics from the beginning, even though new reps will have a ramp period. Tracking metrics is the fastest way to get to a scalable, repeatable sales model.

Metrics fall into two categories: quantitative and qualitative. Under quantitative metrics there are activity metrics, productivity metrics, and conversion rates.

Activity Metrics

Activity metrics are the guidelines for success. Activities lead to results. If you are not achieving the desired results, the root cause may be in the rep activity levels. Without tracking activity levels, it is impossible to understand the cause of the shortfall in results. Activity metrics are leading indicators and predictors of future results.

Productivity Metrics

Productivity metrics measure what reps produce or their results. Quota and commission are based on selected productivity metrics. When reps are not achieving the desired results, the first place to look for a reason is back to the activity metrics. If the activity metrics are on track and they are still not producing the desired results, it may be due to a skills gap. If achievement of results is across a broad set of reps, it may be due to a market shift in terms of demand for your product.

Conversion Rates

Conversion rates enable managers to measure individual rep performance, determine what is working, and identify areas for improvement. These metrics also give reps the ability to understand and prioritize their daily activities.

Conversion rates give sales a sense of where the most deals are falling out of the funnel so steps can be taken to reverse the trend and improve conversion rates.

Finally, conversion rates give sales predictability. If you know your revenue target for a given period and you have reliable conversion rates throughout the sales process, you can work backwards from the target revenue number to understand how many leads must be generated to achieve that number.

Qualitative Metrics

These metrics measure the quality of an activity or the inputs and outputs to sales. For example, a lead rating is an example of a qualitative metric. Whether or not an SQL is accepted by an outside sales rep is also an indication of a qualitative metric.

Qualitative metrics enable improvement in the quality of the output of your organization or request better input. For example, if the rating given to an MQL is lower than the rating allocated by the marketing automation system, it is an opportunity to work with marketing to adjust the lead scoring to better align with what is required for a better quality MQL.

All metric reporting must be real-time and accessible from the sales 2.0 productivity tools being used. Sales reports will only be accurate if usage of these tools is enforced.

Due to the importance of metrics for an inside sales team, they must be looked at frequently. Don't wait until the end of the quarter to view metrics. For an inside sales team, key metrics should be viewed daily, weekly, and monthly. This will allow you to make course corrections quickly and improve the desired results.

An easy-to-access dashboard is the best way to display the reports. Different dashboards can be created to reflect different team, level, or functional responsibilities.

What metrics will you establish and track?

16 Adopt a Sales Methodology

A sales methodology is a common language and set of rules that allows you and your sales reps to communicate about how to move a buyer through the buying process.

You may be wondering what a sales methodology is and how it is different from a sales process, and why you need both.

A sales methodology is a common language and set of rules that allows you and your sales reps to communicate about how to move a buyer through the buying process. Sales methodologies give sales people the tools and training to be able to respond to a buyer in different situations. It enables moving a deal forward and determining what actions to take when a deal gets stuck. It also provides rules for when to walk away from a deal to avoid wasting time on unproductive activities.

A sales methodology requires a sales process (Rule 25) to support it. Knowing how to manage your buyer through the sales stages is provided by the sales methodology.

Dealmaker 365 suggests eight qualities of an effective sales methodology[19]:

1. **Better Qualification and Sales Effectiveness**
    Any good methodology should help your sales team enhance their selling skills, shorten the sales cycle, and close more of the right kinds of deals.

2. **Standard Sales Processes and Common Language**
    Uncommon productivity results when a sales

---

[19] Donal Daly, "8 Steps to Effective Sales Methodology Implementation," *Dealmaker 365* (blog), March 31, 2013, http://sales20network.com/blog/?p=1865.

organization adopts a common way of selling that is understood—not just by the sales team, but also by the rest of the departments that support the sales team. Sales representatives are speaking the same language as sales management. Marketing and customer support understand what is happening in the sales cycle.

3. **Adoption Rate: Ease of Use and Level of Sustained Usage**
   It's important that the sales person uses the sales methodology consistently to achieve real sustained benefit from it.

4. **Leverage Existing Investments: Integrate with Your CRM System**
   The chosen methodology should integrate with the CRM system to amplify the benefits of both. As the sales person works with an opportunity in the CRM system, the methodology should always be present, just where the sales person needs it.

5. **Improve Sales Forecast Accuracy: Know When Deals Will Close**
   Consistent usage of a sales methodology removes much of the subjectivity from assessing when a deal will close.

6. **Gain Control of the Sales Process by Creating Value for the Customer**
   If a sales opportunity is real, the buyer understands the need to change. He or she may not have figured out the transformation that may be necessary. An effective sales person guides him or her through that discovery and demonstrates evidence of the sales person's understanding of the buyer's business and the salesperson's ability to create value for the buyer. The methodology you select should provide your sales team with tools to support them in gaining control of the sale.

7. **Customized to (the Multiple Sales Functions in) Your Business**
   The methodology should to be prescriptive enough to optimize sales effectiveness while being flexible enough to fit your business and related business objectives. A common base methodology can be tailored to reflect the different needs of inside sales and outside sales.

8. **Track Record of the Methodology Vendor's Previous Implementations**
   The success of an implementation is a function of the core methodology, how it is applied to your business, the implementation and after-sales support, as well as the consultants who engage with you. Check out the record of your supplier. Ask about the preparation, the delivery and training, and how well what was implemented is being used, and how it supports the core business objectives.

Which sales methodology will you choose?

17

Arm Your Inside Team with Scripts, Templates, and Professional Collateral

Scripts enable consistent communication by providing speaking points and guidelines for qualifying questions, the company's value proposition, your customer list, and objection handling.

Michael Halper, CEO of SalesScripter, says, "The majority of sales professionals improvise what they say when talking with prospects. Inconsistent communication leads to inconsistent results."[20]

Scripts enable consistent communication by providing speaking points and guidelines for qualifying questions, the company's value proposition, your customer list, and objection handling. Scripts and email templates should be adjusted as the team and products mature and the market changes.

As an example, a voicemail follow-up to a webinar might look something like this:

> Hi, this is Sue with ABC Company. I am following up on a recent webinar you attended. Please call me back at ###-###-#### so we can discuss how our [short description of product] can help [pain] by enabling you to (benefit), like we have successfully done with [Competitor's Company].

Subsequently, we always recommend sending a personal email in conjunction with an initial call attempt. The email mate to this call might look something like this:

> Hello [Name],
>
> Thank you for attending our recent webinar, "[Webinar Title]"

---

[20] SalesScripter, "About Us," *SalesScripter*, October 2013, http://salesscripter.com/about-us/.

Executives like you usually contact us for three reasons:

Some of the biggest planning challenges faced by companies like yours are:

- *Challenge #1*
- *Challenge #2*
- *Challenge #3*

ABC Company enables businesses such as yours to [address one or all of the above challenges].

Please let me know when you have time for a brief discussion.

Regards,
Sue Smith

These are just a few generic examples to get you thinking. Keep in mind that voicemail, conversations, and emails should always be addressing the needs of the prospect/customer—not spitting out features and benefits. Keep your emails brief and to the point. People are very busy and many will be reading your email on a smartphone—you need to quickly capture their interest.

Help make your emails look professional with the appropriate automatic signature. It should include your name, title, company-approved logo, phone number, and personal email address. Provide a hyperlinked company email and social media buttons to facilitate easy engagement. The following point will seem very basic, but be sure your reps have enabled auto-correct in their email settings. There is nothing more unprofessional than an email with obvious spelling errors.

It is best practice to have regular meetings between your sales team that follows up on MQLs and the marketing team that has generated and created the MQL through an offer. Any new marketing campaign should either be reviewed in a meeting or in an email to the sales team that will be following up. Talking points about the campaign should also be drafted by the marketing team to make outreach more targeted.

While the days of printed collateral are gone, people remain hungry for information to educate them and confirm a company's credibility. While you can reference your website, people like having attachments even if a document is featured on your website. Be certain you have at least a one to two page overview of your company and services.

The tools that you provide your inside sales team will provide consistency in your overall messaging to those outside your company.

How do you plan to provide the tools your inside sales team needs to successfully engage with your prospects and customers?

18 Feed the Team

Sales cannot be successful without close alignment with marketing.

Feeding your sales team goes beyond generating leads. It includes a complete sales enablement process. Marketing and sales must be closely aligned on their customer needs, target prospects, their value proposition, and the goals and objectives to which they hold accountable. Sales cannot be successful without close alignment with marketing.

Part of feeding the inside sales team is providing them with a sufficient number of marketing qualified leads (MQLs). The Bridge Group found that, on average, 38 percent of a given inside group's pipeline is generated by marketing.[21] These inbound leads cost 61 percent less than outbound leads.[22] From the company's perspective, marketing should be providing as many inbound leads as possible to sales to maximize the cost effectiveness of the sales process. However, this is dependent upon the budget that is assigned to marketing.

MQLs are the result of numerous marketing activities. Depending on the marketing program and the buyer response, they may or may not be considered an MQL. This is where your marketing au-

---

[21] The Bridge Group, Inc., "SaaS Inside Sales Metrics & Compensation," *The Bridge Group, Inc.*, August 31, 2013, http://www.bridgegroupinc.com/inside_sales_metrics.html.

[22] Melissa Miller, "20 Fresh Stats About the State of Inbound Marketing in 2012," *HubSpot* (blog), February 27, 2012 (9:00 a.m.), http://blog.hubspot.com/blog/tabid/6307/bid/31550/20-Fresh-Stats-About-the-State-of-Inbound-Marketing-in-2012.aspx.

tomation solution comes into place. Based on buyer's match with your target market, interaction with your company and purchasing signals, and the campaign that was responded to by buyers are scored through the marketing automation system. The definition of an MQL should be agreed upon between marketing and sales. Once the score of an MQL is high enough, MQLs are passed to a sales development team. Until that time, they continue to be nurtured by marketing through additional campaigns.

Once they are scored highly enough to be passed to sales development, they are loaded into the CRM system along with their marketing automation score and identified as "hot," "warm," or "cold" to assist the sales development rep in prioritizing their outbound calling effort (Rule 11). The definition of "hot, warm, and cold" should also be agreed upon and used consistently.

When qualifying an MQL, we recommend at least six touches until contact is or is not made.

Once MQLs are qualified, the sales development rep enters their own rating to validate the quality of the auto scoring from the marketing automation system. If the MQL is not rated highly enough by the sales development rep, it is sent back to marketing for additional nurturing. Leads can also be disqualified if there is no future business potential. This is a key part of the collaboration and alignment required between sales and marketing as management meets regularly to discuss campaign performance, lead scoring, and upcoming lead generation events.

When being fed properly by marketing, high-velocity sales development teams positively impact the number of total pipeline opportunities for the sales organization.

The other factor in feeding the team is an ongoing commitment from marketing to provide sales enablement tools. The necessary tools and content are different for each company. A minimum set of sales enablement tools would include the value proposition and messaging, definition of the target audience (including buyer roles, personas and buying motivations), use cases, and ROI. Other critical tools include data sheets, a corporate brochure, request for proposal/information (RFP/RFI) templates, competitive intelligence, campaign briefings, pricing sheets, article reprints, white papers, a product roadmap with reliable timeframes, and initial call and email scripts.

What lead generation mechanisms will you use to feed your inside sales team(s)?

19 Link Compensation to Desired Behaviors

Compensation plans are designed to incent the behavior of the sales reps.

Sales development reps and inside sales reps have different overall objectives. The objective for sales development is to uncover and generate qualified leads that contribute to an increase in the pipeline. The objective for inside sales is to close business. Compensation plans are designed to incent the behavior of the sales reps.

Key components of a general compensation plan include:

- Alignment with the company goals
- Goals that are realistic, considering market conditions and company maturity
- A maximum of three variable components
- Factors that inside sales representatives can control
- Accelerators to incent overachievement
- Monthly payouts

Sales development compensation is aligned with the sales team to which they pass leads—whether that is inside sales or outside sales. Sales development compensation should have two additional components:

- Number of qualified meetings set for sales
- Pipeline contribution or the dollar amount of the qualified leads "accepted" or converted to opportunities by sales

For sales development, the optimal split is 60 percent base and 40 percent variable. The variable portion is divided between the qualified leads quota (75 percent of the variable portion, 30 percent of the total compensation) and the pipeline contribution portion would be the remaining percentage.

Determining whether a qualified lead should be converted into an opportunity is contingent on whether the lead meets the opportunity criteria defined in your company's sales process (Rule 16). As the organization matures, the number of expected qualified meetings will decrease and the pipeline contribution expectations will increase. Compensation plans will have to be adjusted accordingly.

Payment for qualified leads occurs in the month in which the qualified lead is passed, whereas the pipeline contribution portion is paid in the month in which a qualified lead is converted into an opportunity or "accepted" by sales.

Standard compensation components for inside sales reps include a base and a variable component. The variable component is based on a commission plan where the rep receives a percentage of every sale or a quota model where the rep receives a percentage of their variable based on achieving a pre-set number. Compensation elements beyond the standard compensation include spiffs and contests.

For an inside sales team delivering new or upsell business, the split should also be 60 percent base, 40 percent variable. The 40 percent can be entirely based on their revenue quota. If they are teamed with an outside sales organization, 10 percent of their total compensation or 25 percent of the variable portion should be linked to the outside sales rep quota.

Inside sales reps responsible for renewal business will have a base of 70 percent and a variable of 30 percent of their total compensation, the 30 percent being based on their renewal quota.

To incent overachievement, compensation plans should have accelerators that go into effect once they go over one hundred percent of their quota.

Special pay incentives for fast sales (SPIFFS) help keep reps motivated to achieve specific time-based goals. These can be weekly or monthly-based time periods.

All reps should be provided a ramp-up period of at least one quarter, during which time they should be guaranteed their full compensation base plus variable, and paid on any overachievement. Achieving consistent quota production will take another two quarters. After they are fully ramped, reps that miss quota two quarters in a row should be placed on a performance improvement plan (PIP). If results do not improve by the end of the PIP period, the reps must be transitioned out of the business.

Companies may have variations of the above compensation models due to tracking limitations or the desire to drive different behavior. However, the above reflects a "best-practices" approach to compensation.

What are the components of your compensation plans?

20 Incent Inside and Outside Sales to Work Together

You need to decide the rules of engagement (ROE)—the responsibilities of each team, the promotion of working together, and the prevention of resource overlap.

Today, team-selling models make up 51 percent of the inside sales models.[23] If you are building an inside sales team when an outside sales team is already in place, you have to determine if they will work together. You need to decide the rules of engagement (ROE)—the responsibilities of each team, the promotion of working together, and the prevention of resource overlap.

This process starts at the top of the organization. As mentioned in Rule 2, building an inside sales team requires a solid business case and executive management support. This is even more important if you have an outside sales organization that has been in place for years that may not understand the benefits of inside sales and/or feels threatened by the addition of this team.

At the next level, direct managers must be in agreement on how the teams will work together. Both managers have to be able to consistently and clearly articulate the ROE to prevent being pulled into disagreements between sales reps.

ROE include defining the territory or account responsibilities of each team. In a geographic territory-based model, there will typically be a direct correlation between the inside rep and the outside sales rep. With a one-to-one ratio they would cover the same territories. If there are multiple outside reps to inside reps, for example a 3:1 ratio of outside to inside reps, the inside rep would cover three outside territories.

---

[23] Bob Perkins, "The Future of Inside Sales."

Within a territory, there has to be further clarification of responsibilities by either size of an account or size of a deal. There are no specific rules as this depends on your company strategy, target market, target title, product complexity, and average deal size.

As discussed in Rule 19, the compensation in a team model has to encourage teaming and discourage unacceptable behavior. For example, if the inside sales reps only get compensated on deals under a certain size, they may attempt to split a deal to keep it within their payment level. This would be unacceptable behavior. There could be one hundred percent overlap between the quota, or the individual inside sales reps may have a separate quota for their area of responsibility with only a portion of their variable compensation tied to the outside sales quota.

Constant communication within the teams is imperative for success. They have to build a trusting relationship amongst themselves to be successful. Discourage withholding information—it breaks down trust, damages the customer relationship, and negatively impacts the team's overall success.

In teaming situations where we have worked, a qualitative element that has to be taken into consideration are the personalities, strengths and weaknesses of each inside sales rep, and the outside rep(s) with whom they are teamed. The personalities have to click and the capabilities between the inside rep and the outside rep should be complimentary. This makes territory assignment more complicated but getting it right creates an unbeatable synergy.

A teamed selling model is what the company decided upon when the first time I built an inside sales organization. Outside sales had been the primary sales channel for years. The outside team was already uncomfortable knowing an inside sales team was being built. The teams had to work together and the best way to get that to happen and encourage acceptance of the inside team was to start with a team selling quota. Although we did not get immediate buy-in from outside sales, once they knew their compensation would not be negatively impacted, they were willing to give the inside team a try. As relationships were built, sales dramatically increased and success stories were tracked—we were able to get buy-in from the outside team. We had individual outside reps stand up at sales meetings and give testimonials on how working with their inside counterparts were a winning combination.

What steps will you take to ensure effective teaming between your inside and outside teams?

Section III
Leading and Managing

Now that you have your personnel resources in place, effective leadership and management are critical to ensure their success.

21

Motivate with Contests

The key to creating a contest is to make sure the goal is achievable by all team members.

One of the best ways to drive performance (while boosting morale) is through contests. Contests bring out the competitive nature of your inside sales team. The contests don't have to be complicated nor cost a lot of money. In fact, paid time off (full or half day) can be a great motivator for hard workers.

The key to creating a contest is to make sure the goal is achievable by all team members. If the competition is not motivating, it can fall flat. Contests can take place for short periods of time, maybe a two-hour call blitz, or they can occur over an extended period of time, a month or even a quarter to promote a new product or process. It is advised to carefully choose a timeframe for your contest that is sustainable as inside sales reps could start to burn out performing at high levels.

When considering contests, individual competition generally comes to mind. Some examples of individual contests are:

- A random, daily cash giveaway. Select a metric, such as three new leads for the day. The prize for the first rep to get to that goal is $50 cash.

- The sales person that has the most month-to-month sales increase gets a paid Friday off.

- Have a raffle with a grand prize, such as a sizable gift card. If you are trying to acquire new customers, give a raffle ticket to the rep when they close an opportunity. The more new customers, the better their chance of winning.

- Call blitz. Walk around your sales floor and hand out lottery tickets as you hear reps engaging in valuable sales conversations.

Team contests can also be motivating and very successful. This is easier to facilitate if your team is centralized. Some examples of a team contest are:

- Set a monthly activity quota, maybe for a new product introduction, that is aligned with the company's goals. If the goal is met, the team can go bowling or to a professional sporting event.

- If your team is large enough, split the reps into teams and have them compete against each other. For each new customer, they get a point. The team with the highest number of points at the end of the month gets a free lunch outing.

Recently, gamification has become a popular part of the Sales 2.0 landscape. Gamification seeks to engage employees with a real-time reward structure that includes a level of competition. Gamification applications are a perfect fit for the newest generation in the workforce, who are referred to as "Millennials." They have grown up with video games and electronic devices so it directly addresses to how they will most likely engage in the working world.

Gamification may not be an investment that you make when first building a team but it is something to keep in mind as another way to motivate your team. It is important to note that there are some free gamification applications available on the market, provided that you have the personnel resources for the implementation.

The key to successful contests and gamification is to make it fun! Get creative, have fun, and even involve your team in planning. They know best what would give them additional motivation.

What contests will you run to motivate your inside sales team?

Inspire, Coach, and Mentor

Inspiring people requires having a passion for helping others' succeed, a love for what you are doing, and leading by example.

Creating the "buzz" that exists within high-velocity inside sales teams requires executive commitment. This includes encouraging and supporting their efforts by posting results in company-wide forums and communicating results to the entire organization, developing both the team as a whole and each individual by rewarding outstanding results.

In order to realize the results that you are looking for, each rep requires a unique approach to coaching and mentoring.

One night while I was working I heard one of our recently promoted reps on the phone. Previously, he had sold for our small business team and his promotion was to our mid-market team. As I listened to him on the phone, I was surprised that the management team had promoted him. His phone skills were poor and needed development. I spoke to the direct manager about the new rep training process and about providing this rep with some individualized training. Realistically, the manger did not have the bandwidth to provide the level of individualized training required for this employee. This is an unfortunate problem that many sales leaders face, not having the time to provide the level of coaching required for their reps.

Every night this rep stayed late, making call after call. It was clear he had the drive and foundational skills to be a more skilled inside sales representative. In order to mitigate the bandwidth problem we leveraged an outside sales trainer, Josiane Feigon, President of TeleSmart Communications, to provide one-on-one coaching for this particular rep.

Josiane spent time with this rep, listening to his calls and providing feedback on how he could improve. She also worked with him to role-play real-life sales scenarios so that he would be comfortable handling these situations when they came up with prospects and customers.

This investment paid off handsomely. He was so appreciative and inspired by the investment we made in him that he became one of that team's top producers.

Ingrid Steinbergs, Worldwide Vice President, Inside Sales at Hewlett-Packard, shared another story with me.

> On my first day at another software company, where I was leading a team of 12 inside reps, I was told to feel free to 'fire' any of the reps. The reasoning was the previous director was in a 'hurry' to hire and therefore, 'We may have made some bad choices.' There was one rep in particular who was really struggling ... he had been onboard for less than three months, and had no coaching. His morale was down and he felt like quitting. As I sat with him and did side-by-side coaching, I saw a passion in him to succeed. I made it my mission to spend an hour each day, for two weeks straight, coaching him. I am very pleased to say he became my top rep for the year. Many of the execs shook their heads in wonder ... how did our lowest-performing rep become our top-performing rep?
>
> Coaching is not only mandatory. It works![24]

Ideally, each inside sales representative should have an individual development plan so that their manager understands their career goals and the rep understands what steps he or she has to take to achieve these goals. It is the rep's responsibility to design the plan and then it should be discussed and agreed upon in his or her annual performance review meeting. Managers can perform quarterly updates with the rep to discuss progress against the plan.

Inspiring people requires having a passion for helping others' succeed, a love for what you are doing, and leading by example. When you emote that kind of passion and excitement, it becomes contagious and infectious to others. When you take the time to individualize your coaching and mentoring, reps know that you care about them as individuals and will put in the effort to deliver the best results possible. This approach takes more time but it is returned to you in spades.

What techniques will you use to inspire your team?

---

[24] Ingrid Steinbergs, email message to Lori Harmon , September 22, 2013.

23 Use and Monitor Social Media

The buyer's journey is changing and we want to be there, where the buyer is.

Today, social media is a required tool for all sales professionals. Something once thought to be a distraction is now an essential part of an inside sales person's success. According to research by the Aberdeen Group, 46 percent of sales people incorporating social into their sales process make quota versus 38 percent who achieve quota without the use of social selling.[25]

One of the best examples of inside sales success using social selling is at ADP. The inside sales team at ADP is led by Liz Gelb-O'Connor, Vice President of Inside Sales Strategy and Growth. According to Liz, "The buyer's journey is changing and we want to be there, where the buyer is."[26] Today, buyers are using their contacts, the Internet, and social media to make purchasing decisions. A 2012 study by the Corporate Executive Board found that the average B2B purchase decision is 57 percent complete by the time a supplier is engaged.[27]

In order to be where the buyer is, ADP has provided their inside sales team with the social me-

---

[25] Aberdeen Group, "Collaborate, Listen, Contribute: How Best-in-Class Sales Teams Leverage Social Selling," *Aberdeen Group*, November 2012, http://www.aberdeen.com/Aberdeen-Library/8256/RB-social-selling-intelligence.aspx.

[26] Liz Gelb-O'Connor, email message to Lori Harmon, September 30, 2013.

[27] "Sell How Your Customers Want to Buy," *CEB*, accessed August 31, 2013, http://www.executiveboard.com/exbd/sales-service/challenger/new-decision-timeline/index.page.

dia tools required to be on the forefront of social selling. This has enabled Liz's team to shape customer demand and position themselves as thought leaders in the industry.

An example of this thought leadership is that one of the managers at ADP closed a deal by answering a question posed in a LinkedIn group. The manager noticed a discussion about pre-employment drug testing. He took the opportunity to share his knowledge with the LinkedIn Group. Even though he identified himself as working for ADP he did not attempt to sell any products in his post. Later, he received an email from the person that posted the question asking for a meeting with ADP to learn about their services regarding pre-employment. Within two weeks he closed a deal with this client.

Be sure your inside sales reps are on the social media sites where your customers and buyers are—be it LinkedIn, Twitter, Facebook, Google+, etc. Provide them with relevant content to share and train them on how to engage and participate in conversations. Publish, share best practices, incent participation, and track results.

Which social media forum is best for your particular product or service? It depends.

Sixty-five percent of business-to-business (B2B) companies have acquired a customer through LinkedIn.[28] There are numerous ways your inside sales team can leverage LinkedIn. First, their profile should be customer-centric. Rep profiles should be a reflection of what they have accomplished in helping their customers. Also, they should become members of relevant groups in order to participate in discussions and give advice to those looking for solutions that your product or service addresses. LinkedIn can also be used to broker introductions. If you know someone who has a connection in an account where your company is looking to gain traction or engage as a prospect, ask for a referral.

We recently worked with a client who had had a LinkedIn profile for years but was an infrequent user. Two months after we trained him on a best-practices LinkedIn approach, he closed a $150,000 deal through one of his new connections.

For businesses-to-consumer (B2C) companies, 77 percent have found leads on Facebook, as it is a more personal networking platform.[29] These are only two social media platforms. We have provided a list of other platforms and tools in Appendix D. The most successful companies utilize multiple social media tools to reach their buyers.

How do you plan to incorporate social media into your sales strategy?

---

[28] Melissa Miller, "20 Fresh Stats About the State of Inbound Marketing in 2012."
[29] Ibid.

Smart Cold Calling Works

Cold calling is not a current best practice. But, with the rise of relationship selling and social media, it is possible to make cold calling productive.

To cold call, or not to cold call: that is the hotly debated question. While it takes a considerable amount of time with a far lower return on investment, it is often necessary to fill the gap that exists between the number of MQL opportunities and the pipeline development necessary to meet sales goals.

Cold calling—in the traditional sense—is not a current best practice. But, with the rise of relationship selling and social media, it is possible to work smarter—not necessarily harder—to make cold calling more productive.

If you have your reps following up on warm leads and cold calling, it is likely that most will procrastinate on cold calling. Sales reps simply don't like making cold calls.

In one company where I worked, the sales organization at the time was structured as such that outside sales was responsible for one hundred named (enterprise) accounts per rep while the inside sales team was responsible for everything else.

The marketing team generated a sufficient number of MQLs, but the vast majority was not to the larger, enterprise-sized accounts that were handled by the outside sales team. Outside sales became dissatisfied, feeling that their pipelines were suffering.

Our solution was to take two highly skilled, more senior sales development reps that had proven ability to penetrate larger accounts and reduced their quota—it's obviously harder to get a lead from cold call efforts. We teamed them with multiple outside reps; they had weekly calls, and were given 10 accounts to pursue that week. The SDRs were able to get results by securing meetings in targeted accounts where the outside reps needed introductions to build their funnel.

In another situation, one of my more ambitious reps took it upon herself to do cold calling for her outside counterpart because MQLs were anemic and she had a quota. She called and emailed a key executive at a marquee retail account that turned into a small pilot. The pilot then turned into a multimillion dollar account!

Gone are the days of dialing for dollars. If you are going to cold call, you need to leverage whatever tools are available to help you get a foot in the door. Your target accounts need to be clearly defined. Then, utilize a tool, such as LinkedIn, to see if you can broker a referral. This is far more effective than traditional "cold" calls (Rule 23).

Researching the company and the person you are trying to contact in advance of your outreach is expected and the only way to have the information needed to make a connection with your target contact. In order to leave a voicemail that gets the prospect's attention or engage in a conversation, reps must have knowledge of what the prospect or their company is trying to accomplish and be able to link that to your company's solution.

Finally, having a positive attitude—like that demonstrated by the ambitious rep described above—is imperative for cold calling. A rep's attitude and confidence will come through during his or her call.

How will you use cold calling strategically?

25 Closely Manage Your Deals

A sales process is a time-based series of clearly defined stages that a deal must pass through in order to close and generate revenue for the company.

Once a qualified lead becomes an opportunity (a deal that has been entered into the sales cycle), the inside sales rep has to take the opportunity through a sales process. A sales process is a time-based series of clearly defined stages that a deal must pass through in order to close and generate revenue for the company. The sales process should be mapped closely to the buyer's purchasing process. More recently, companies have begun referring to their sales process as the buying process.

In order for everyone to understand where a deal or opportunity is in the sales process, each sales stage should have clear entry point and buyer-related exit criteria. Each sales stage has buyer-specific steps that are to be completed, to indicate a deal has moved to the next stage.

Below is an example of a generic sales process. Note that a sales process is unique to each company and should be customized accordingly. Differences will be based on target verticals, products offered, complexity of the products, and buying cycle.

Stage 0 is the qualification stage, typically owned by the sales development team. The contact here is still considered a lead versus an opportunity. Once the criteria for Stage 0 have been met, the lead is converted to an opportunity. Stage 1 is the beginning of a sale cycle and it is now considered part of a sales rep's pipeline. The pipeline is the set of deals a rep has that have some probability of closing. The closing probability for each sales stage is listed at the bottom of each column in the chart below.

Stage 0	Stage 1	Stage 2	Stage 3	Stage 4	Stage 5	Stage 6
Suspect	Prospect Validation	Develop	Evaluation	Business Negotiation	Contract Process	Closed Won
• To be qualified • Contact established • Qualification criteria identified	• Decision maker and process identified • Driving business issue understood and is a match with product • Competition identified	• Action plan agreed to in writing to move forward • Technical requirements established • Budget identified	• Executive involvement • Technical evaluation successfully completed • Received approval to spend budget	• References provided and contacted • Pricing and terms submitted • Buyer gives verbal award	• Terms negotiated • Redline received • Number of days for PO/Contract confirmed	• Customer PO number on record • Confirmation of receipt of PO from partner
Qualified Suspect	Initial Meeting	Success Criteria	Preferred	Verbal Win	PO Received	Won
10%	15%	25%	50%	75%	90%	100%

In order to support and teach your inside sales reps how to move a deal through the sales process and ensure accurate forecasting (Rule 26), management must adhere to these stages and the associated terminology when discussing deals. Deals should only move to the next sales stage when all of the buyer actions have been completed and the exit criteria have been met.

CRM systems, like Salesforce.com, SugarCRM, Microsoft Dynamics, or any other CRM of your choice, can and should be customized to reflect your company's specific sales cycle. Then, the sales cycle progress should be tracked in your CRM system as deals move through the different stages.

As deals are going through the sales process, some will be won and some will be lost. It is just as important to know why you won as to know why you lost, so this information should be tracked. When opportunities are marked "Closed Lost" in your CRM system, the rep should also be required to enter a "Lost Reason Code." Examples of lost reason codes include: competition and the requirement to enter the name of the competitor, pricing, company restructuring, or loss of funding. These can also be customized in any CRM system. A key way to win more deals is to understand why you lost and adjust accordingly, assuming the reason is something that your company can control, and is in line with your overall company strategy.

What are the steps in your sales process?

26 Forecast Accurately

In order to forecast accurately, your forecasting process requires its own methodology.

Forecast accuracy is critically important to companies regardless of size, industry, and/or whether they are public or private. It has been reported as one of companies' top two challenges.[30] Public companies need accurate forecasts to report to Wall Street. For pre-IPO companies, forecast accuracy gives the board confidence in the management team.

Accurate forecasting requires its own methodology. Many companies forecast utilizing a probability model. They multiply the value of their deals by the probability that the deal will close. For example, if you have five deals totaling $100,000 with a 40 percent probability of closing, two deals totaling $50,000 with a probability of 75 percent of closing and six deals totaling $200,000 with a 90 percent probability of closing your forecast would be as follows.

$100,000 x .4 = 40,000
$50,000 x .75 = 37,500
$200,000 x .90 = 180,000

Total forecast: $275,500

Forecasting using the probability method often results in an inaccurate forecast, especially with larger deals. A deal is either going to close or it is not. The deal closes and the company receives $100,000 or it does not close and the company receives $0.

A more accurate methodology is for the sales manager to review the key deals with each rep and have them update their deals in the CRM to reflect the

---

[30] The Bridge Group Inc., "Lead Generation Metrics & Compensation."

correct sales stage (Rule 25) and commitment level. Commitment levels are terms used to describe the confidence a sales person has on the probability of a deal closing within a specified quarter based on their knowledge of the buyer process.

"Commit" deals for the quarter are expected to close in the current quarter. "Upside" deals may or may not close during the current quarter. "Pipeline" deals are all deals available to close in a specified quarter.

In our model the commitment level is separate from the sales stage and probability. A deal can be in commit or upside at any stage starting with Stage 2. Timing of a deal closing is based on the sales rep's understanding of when the deal will close based on where their buyer is in the buying process.

Once deals are accurately reflected in the CRM, the forecast becomes:

Closed Won Deals + Committed Deals + Management Adjustment

Management adjustment is the total amount of deals in the upside that the sales manager believes will close during the current quarter. This decision is based on conversations with the sales reps. A deal is put in commit early in the sales process opens a dialogue to fully vet where the deal is in the process. The forecast dollar amount is the actual total forecasted dollar amount of the deals that fit into the above formula. It is not the probability method of multiplying deals by their probability of closing and totaling them.

Stage 0	Stage 1	Stage 2	Stage 3	Stage 4	Stage 5	Stage 6
Suspect	Prospect Validation	Develop	Evaluation	Business Negotiation	Contract Process	Closed Won
		← Current Quarter Pipeline →				
					Forecast	
		Commit or Upside				Commit
Qualified Suspect	Initial Meeting	Success Criteria Established	Pre-Award	Verbal Win	PO Received	Booked Deal
10%	15%	25%	50%	75%	90%	100%

In my experience, forecasting specific deals using a combination of sales stage, commitment level, and a conversation with a sales rep provides the most accurate forecast. It takes a few quarters for everyone to develop a consistent interpretation of where a deal is in the sales process, making a sales process where everyone speaks the same language critical to forecast accuracy.

At one company, we improved forecast accuracy to 98 percent accurate from 63 percent accurate over a two-year period using this methodology.

How will you calculate your forecast?

27 Maximize Your Recurring Revenue

A company using a best-practices approach can generate 30 percent to 40 percent of their total revenue from recurring revenue.

Recurring revenue is your most profitable source of revenue. It costs six to seven times more to acquire a new customer than to retain an existing one,[31] making it critical to stay engaged with your customers after the initial sale.

On average, companies leave 15 percent of their recurring revenue on the table.[32] For major technology companies, that equals nearly $30 billion of lost revenue.[33] Until you gain complete insight into existing customers, you're leaving money on the table by sub-optimizing your renewals process, including cross-sell or upsell opportunities. A company using a best-practices approach can generate 30 percent to 40 percent of their total revenue from recurring revenue. This revenue is the most profitable revenue for companies typically delivering 50 percent in profit.[34] This is profit that can be invested in developing new products.

Not employing a best-practices renewal process leads to sales inefficiencies and missed renewal opportunities. Nearly 45 percent of customers do not renew because of "no contact." It may be for

---

[31] "Recurring Revenue: Five Secrets to Fly High and Fuel Growth," ServiceSource, http://img.en25.com/Web/srev/%7B529cb152-b5d9-4d8c-b3c3-5c585e0b8dd4%7D_5_Secrets_ebook_2013.pdf.

[32] Randy Brasche, email message to Lori Harmon, September 17, 2013.

[33] "Drive Revenue from Renewals: Why Is Recurring Revenue Important?", ServiceSource, September 1, 2013 http://www.servicesource.com/sites/default/files/S8S256011.pdf.

[34] Ibid, email.

lack of data, lack of coverage, a call not received or returned, or a number of other reasons.[35] And, recurring revenue is a perishable asset: renewal rates decline by 3 percent each week after a contract expires. Once a contract is 30 days past expiration, renewal rates are typically cut in half.[36]

Finally, data quality is the biggest culprit for lost recurring revenue. Most companies rely upon data from multiple systems to generate renewal quotes. This data spans contracts, assets, customer information, sales orders, entitlements, and more. Additionally, this data is often outdated, incorrect, or missing. As a result, sales teams waste precious time piecing together information for a renewal quote, while missing critical information to effectively capture recurring revenue.

According to ServiceSource International, the world's leader in recurring revenue management, there are five best practices for maximizing your recurring revenue.[37] These rules apply to any technology company specializing in hardware, software, SaaS, healthcare, life sciences, and industrial.

- Start with the renewal facts: understand the role of recurring revenue on your bottom line. What is your company's true renewal potential?
- Get your data renewal-ready: enhance and centralize your renewal data to gain a complete and accurate picture of your renewal opportunity.
- Create actionable analytics: know how many contracts renew before expiration.
- Manage your channel partners to significantly increase recurring revenue: give channel partners access to the KPI data needed to run their renewal business, and provide comparative data against other partners.
- Develop a culture of selling discipline and precision: create specialization for key renewal sales functions. Only 21 percent of companies have a dedicated renewals sales team. It takes one hundred hours of training within the first year to build a recurring revenue sales expert.

Recurring revenue is growing at 8 percent per year and compounds over time, while new revenue grows at 6 percent per year.[38] A company must increase customer lifetime value to realize recurring. Whether you are renewing maintenance and support, software licenses, subscriptions, or a combination, mastering recurring revenue drives higher revenues, profits, and higher customer retention.

How do you plan to maximize your recurring revenue?

---

[35] Ibid, ebook, pg 36.
[36] Ibid. ebook, pg 14.
[37] "Recurring Revenue: Five Secrets to Fly High and Fuel Growth."
[38] Ibid.

28 Know How to Manage Quotas

Motivated, dedicated sales reps should be able to meet or exceed their quota.

An essential and significant part of your inside sales team's pay will likely be tied to variable compensation. Philosophies on setting quotas vary. Being that they are meant to be an incentive, it is best that quotas be set so that they are challenging but attainable. Motivated, dedicated sales reps should be able to meet or exceed their quota.

Quota setting should be thoroughly thought through. It should take into consideration the overall revenue goals of the company and the role of the inside sales rep.

Are quotas being set for a sales development rep? Then you will be giving both a qualified meeting and a pipeline contribution quota. The qualified meetings quota is derived by starting with the company revenue targets, determining the MQLs that will be delivered, and the conversion rate from MQL to SQL. There should also be a number of qualified meetings resulting from outbound prospecting factored into the total qualified meetings quota. The pipeline contribution quota is calculated by taking the SQL to opportunity conversion rate to determine the number of opportunities originating from sales development that were added to the pipeline.

When setting quotas for inside sales relative to how much business they are required to close, you have to consider different factors. Start with the amount of company revenue they are responsible for generating. Then, add the over-assignment from the company revenue down to the rep level. To divide this between multiple reps, their individual territory differences will have to be considered.

If your inside sales team is partnered with outside sales, use your ROE (Rule 20) to determine how quotas should be set.

For all different types of inside sales reps, a ramp time should be factored in when setting their quota. Seasonality and quarterly revenue percentages should also be included.

At times, despite the best intentions, quotas, in the form of leads or dollar attainments, may need to be adjusted.

At one company where I worked, sales rep turnover was 45 percent. Turnover is an expensive process, regardless of the circumstances (Rule 32). In this situation, over-assignment from the company revenue goals to the individual reps were 25 percent. The reps were at most four management levels down from the CEO. In other words, under the CEO was (1) an EVP of Worldwide Sales, (2) a VP of Inside Sales and several (3) Inside Sales Directors. Then, there were (4) the reps. As a rule, over assignments are 2 percent to 3 percent per management level. So at the most, these over-assignments should have been no more than 12 percent. Not a single sales person was able to attain their quota, resulting in the 45 percent turnover. Once we adjusted the over-assignment and reset the quotas, turnover decreased to 25 percent. The company still had a sufficient over-assignment and easily attained their revenue numbers.

Although not quite as common, sometimes quotas are set too low. This could mean several things. Maybe your team is highly motivated and excelling (not a bad situation). If you have budgeted correctly, it may not be wise to disrupt the momentum until the term of the commission contract is complete.

Of course, every year quotas are redone and adjusted according to the growth estimates of the company. Any seasoned sales person rarely expects their quota to do anything other than increase year over year. If you have junior reps, you may need to discuss this with them when you are giving them their new plan.

How will you know if your team's quotas are set properly?

29 Money Isn't the Only Motivator

The lack of advancement opportunity is often cited as a reason for employees to go elsewhere after a short tenure.

Sales people are motivated by money. While it is important, other factors come into play when hiring and retaining good talent. In sales there is always the combination of base and variable. But that isn't all.

Other items employees consider when comparing to other companies in your area include:

- Medical/dental/insurance benefits
- Paid time off
- Stock options
- Tuition reimbursement or supplemental training
- Work hours
- Career path
- Individual motivation
- Company culture

Benefits are considered to be a part of any employee's overall employment package. If you have an HR person or department, they are likely to have information on how your company compares to similar companies in your market and geographic area. If not, then it is important that you be knowledgeable so that you can be informed when addressing prospective employees or keeping the ones that you have.

Generally, employers provide medical/dental/insurance benefits, although there are variations that will be considered. Is it employee only? What is the employee contribution? Are domestic partners covered? Paid time, and vacation and sick time can also vary between companies. Most companies provide a minimum of two weeks annual vacation but they may also reward employees by giving them additional time off for tenure. Stock options are fairly typical for start-ups and can be an income consideration for companies that may not be able to compete when it comes to wages. Likely, but of less importance than the others, is whether your company provides any type of tuition reimbursement.

Alternative work hours are sometimes difficult in traditional work environments. For companies that have an inside sales team with nationwide coverage, this can be a benefit. In the San Francisco Bay Area, it is common and desirable for reps covering East Coast territories to work East Coast hours to avoid traffic congestion.

A key consideration with the shortage of experienced inside sales talent in today's market is if you have a stated career path. Sales development and inside sales are often considered entry-level sales positions leading to more lucrative roles in the organization. They are likely to want to put in extra effort if they know it could result in advancement. In my experience, the lack of advancement opportunity is often cited as a reason for employees to go elsewhere after a short tenure.

Working with your employees to understand their individual inner motivation and working with them to develop and tap into that motivation can be the best motivator. That motivation may be their career path, it may be being the top rep, or something else. Treating reps as individuals and working with them on their unique internal motivation can result in highly motivated employees.

Also examine subjective things like the overall work environment. While these elements are often hard to identify and difficult to change, improving a person's work environment and the people they work with can be a tremendous motivator. Is it a place where people like to come to work every day for 8+ hours? Portals such as Glassdoor (http://www.glassdoor.com/) have become popular go-to places for job seekers. If your own employees don't feel happy and rewarded, you can easily get an unfavorable reputation. This can adversely impact your ability to attract and retain good talent.

What ideas do you have for motivating your inside sales team?

30 Avoid Time Wasters

Sixty-five percent of a sales rep's time is spent on activities that don't generate new sales.

Lori Rush, Cyber Security Software sales executive, says, "We have four year ends. Because quotas are set on a quarterly basis, Sales is responsible for delivering results, quarter after quarter. When the quarter is completed, we start all over again. With this responsibility and the limited time available in a quarter, activities that waste time must be avoided." Yet, according to Velocify, "65 percent of a sales rep's time is spent on activities that don't generate new sales."[39]

With only 215 selling days in a year, sales management has to be very conscious that they, the executive management team, and other functional groups do not create time wasters for their sales team. The individual reps have to stick to the time-management principles covered in Rule 30 and push back on unnecessary interruptions.

The largest single time waster is an unqualified prospect. Make sure your reps are adhering to the lead qualification criteria established for your company (Rule 9) so that they are not spending time on or passing unqualified leads. Continuing to have meetings with unqualified prospects takes a sales person away from spending time with qualified prospects and moving deals forward in the sales process.

---

[39] Velocity, "The Ultimate Contact Strategy: The Ultimate Contact Strategy: How to Best Use Phone and Email for Contact and Conversion Success." *Velocify*, September 1, 2013 http://www.velocify.com/resources/whitepapers/whitepaper-download/?msg=whitepaper&KW=UCS12&wp=100.

Meetings are another big time waster. We recommend certain meetings in Rule 31. In a best-practices environment meetings should be limited to two hours per week and scheduled outside of the optimal calling hours. This means if there is an important company meeting one week; another regular meeting may have to be cancelled. It also requires meetings to be run efficiently and on time.

Whenever possible, represent your team at meetings with other functional groups. Most other groups are not sensitive to wasting valuable sales time and will not appreciate the impact unless you explain it to them. Often sales is invited to meetings that have no value to them, so these should be declined or prescreened by management.

Then there are the requests for manual reporting that comes from executive management or marketing. Because these requests come from senior management they are usually prioritized over other sales-generating activities. It is the manager's responsibility to push back and protect sales teams from these requests. Manual reporting can be eliminated by automation of the metrics and reports described in Rule 13.

Requesting sales to clean up the contacts and/or leads in the CRM is a very time-consuming task. This typically is the result of loading leads into the CRM that should never have been put there in the first place—raw leads, inquiries not meeting the MQL standard, purchased lists, or lists from a sales person's Rolodex. Renewal sales people spend **less than 45 percent** of their time selling,[40] largely because they are gathering, cleaning, and prepping data for calls. According to Gartner, poor data quality is a primary reason that **40 percent** of all business initiatives fail to achieve their targeted benefits.[41]

Then there are the individual conversations, "water cooler" type chats with colleagues. We were involved in a situation where a sales rep was a significant time waster of their and others' time. It was impossible to have a short conversation with this particular rep. He would say, "Can I have five minutes of your time?" If you were not careful, 20 minutes later, he would still be talking. Even during the quarter end push, he was still talking. To get that situation under control, I wrapped caution tape around his cube with a sign saying, "It is quarter end, do not talk to me." It was an extreme situation requiring extreme measures. But it worked and got the point across.

What will you do to help your team avoid time wasters?

---

[40] Margot Schmorak, "3 Steps to Getting Your Customer Data Clean and Lean," *ServiceSource* (blog), September 9, 2013, http://blog.servicesource.com/2013/09/3-steps-to-getting-your-customer-data-clean-and-lean/.

[41] Ted Friedman and Michael Smith, "Measuring the Business Value of Data Quality," *Gartner*, October 10, 2011, http://www.data.com/export/sites/data/common/assets/pdf/DS_Gartner.pdf.

31

Run Effective Meetings

A sales manager has to be an effective meeting planner, organizer, and leader.

Meetings can take up so much of our time because there can be so many excuses to have them. This is the way we make decisions and often collaborate. In sales they can be huge time wasters that we want to avoid (Rule 30).

To maximize the effectiveness of meetings for your team, a sales manager has to be an effective meeting planner, organizer, and leader. Set an agenda with specific times for each topic and stick to it. If you are doing a by person forecast update and each rep has three minutes, stop them when they have used up their three minutes and have the rest of the conversation one-on-one so they are not taking time away from the other reps. Train and expect your reps to come to meetings prepared and able to efficiently explain key updates and points to their forecast.

Here are the steps to running an effective inside sales meeting.

* Establish a goal for the meeting. What do you want to accomplish? One example for an inside sales team is: perform a forecast review or practice uncovering the prospect's pain. Meetings and training events are both forms of meetings. Often people have meetings with no objective or agenda set so they are unproductive. Yet training sessions nearly always have an agenda.
* Determine what topics have to be covered during the meeting to achieve the goal.

- Based on the topics, figure out how much time the meeting will take to complete. Obviously, the shorter the better, from a sales perspective.
- Assign owners to the agenda items.
- Communicate prior to the meeting. Compose an email that states the goal of the meeting and lists the agenda items with timeframes for each item and who owns the item. If appropriate, solicit input for other agenda items before the meeting so they don't pop up during the meeting and possibly derail the discussion.
- Once the agenda is complete, distribute it at least 24 hours in advance; sooner if individuals will be required to prepare to lead the topics that they own.
- Get to the meeting a few minutes early as you are leading by example—so don't be late!
- Start the meeting on time even if all of the attendees are not present. It is important to respect the time of the individuals that did show up on time. Again, leading by example, you will be demonstrating that being prompt is critical and part of working together as a team.
- When you start the meeting, review the goals of the meeting and the agenda, and then start the discussion.
- Keep the meeting running smoothly; start and end each topic based on the times allocated by the agenda.
- If there is a conversation or people are taking turns speaking, help to keep them on track. If it is a presentation or a longer meeting, give them a five-minute warning that their time is nearly finished. In shorter meetings, you will have to end the topic and pick up any remaining items in a separate meeting.

Over time, people will understand that timeliness is important to you and most will learn to adhere to established timeframes. They will also learn how to better manage their time and their meetings with prospects. Additionally, you will keep them focused on what is the most important time—selling time.

Share this rule with colleagues and other cross-functional teams that invite you and your team to meetings that drag on and take away from valuable sales time.

How do you plan to conduct efficient, effective inside sales meetings?

32 | Know the Cost of a Bad Hire

The costs associated with a bad hire are not simply monetary.

A Career Builder study states, "66 percent of U.S. employers say they have been affected by bad hires in the last year."[42] While a company-wide statistic, this is of particular concern in a sales organization.

Finding the right talent to meet your needs can be a challenge. You may feel rushed to fill a position to avoid falling behind on certain goals. Don't settle and hire someone based on the fact that "they could do the job."

The costs associated with a bad hire are not simply monetary (see material referenced below if you want to quote a dollar figure). There is the loss of productivity and management time spent as a result of an underperforming individual. It also exposes the company to potential legal and human resource issues. Inside sales teams are tribal, so a bad hire can be toxic to your team. It can disrupt and distract peers from their day-to-day responsibilities.

I worked with a company that had a long-term employee hired for a particular role. Over time, his job changed multiple times as the company evolved. He flew under the radar because each quarter he would produce the exact number of qualified leads required to meet his target. How-

---

[42] Mary Lorenz, "What's the Cost of a Bad Hire? A Global Perspective," *The Hiring Site* (*CareerBuilder* blog), May 8, 2013, http://thehiringsite.careerbuilder.com/2013/05/08/whats-the-cost-of-a-bad-hire-a-global-perspective/.

ever, he thought he knew everything. He continually shared his "knowledge" with his peers, whether they wanted to hear it or not. His constant talking was disruptive to everyone's workflow. Management knew that he was not a good fit but were afraid to let him go as they were fearful of missing their numbers.

After consulting with an outside expert, management implemented a best-practices approach where call and email activities (along with results-oriented success metrics) were implemented. The activities of this particular rep were far below industry averages. He was capable of producing better results if he could stop talking and start working. His talking also prevented others from performing their daily activities.

Setting appropriate activity (such as number of outbound calls and emails) levels enabled management to set a higher qualified lead quota and gain visibility into the negative impact of this bad hire. Even when a rep is achieving their "objectives," they can still be a bad hire.

Although you can never be guaranteed to hire correctly all the time there are a few actions that you can take to minimize the risk.

- Ask for referrals if you find a mutual connection (for example, through LinkedIn). Why wouldn't you do the same for your work environment?
- Have several team or company members interview the candidate so that you can compare notes and, more importantly, possible warning signs.
- Role-play during the interview process—mock calls and voicemails, asking them to send you prospecting emails.
- Make sure the interview process is consistent.
- Always check references personally! Do not leave reference checking up to Human Resources. Inside sales managers who are peers are more likely to open up to you than to Human Resources who may use a standard list of questions. You may ask different questions based on the responses of the references with whom you are speaking. Regardless of how crunched you are for time or how urgently you need to fill the position, do not overlook this key part of the hiring process.
- Invest in a background check if one is not currently standard hiring practice for your company. Resume fraud does occur and it is wise to know of any integrity gaps in advance of the hire.

How will you ensure that you avoid making a hiring mistake?

33 Develop an Ongoing Talent Pool

Always be recruiting. You need to prepare for open headcount at all times.

As a sales manager, you want to find the best talent in the shortest time possible and secure that talent. That is difficult to do if you are not developing an ongoing talent pool.

Start by retaining the reps that you have by providing them with a career path. Extra effort and a job well done should be rewarded to reduce the chance of a gap being created within your inside sales team.

If your inside team is primarily a sales development team, the general expectation is 12 to 18 months of success in a role before receiving a promotion. Therefore, depending upon when your reps were hired, you may find yourself with multiple positions open at any given time. Open positions may also coincide with an expansion, with turnover, and/or with multiple promotions. You may also have openings due to a bad hire or a poor performer.

David Sterenfeld of Corporate Dynamix advised me, "Always be recruiting."[43] You need to prepare for open headcount at all times. Maybe you have recently filled a position. That being the case, perhaps you were fortunate to have to choose between multiple qualified candidates. I have found this to be an exceptional case, though.

As an inside sales leader, my best source of candidates has been through my professional network. Additionally, I maintained relationships with key re-

---

[43] David Sterenfeld (Corporate Dynamix) in discussion with Debbi Funk, July 2013.

cruiters who were well networked. In urgent situations, these recruiters' ability to quickly launch a search and fill an open position was key to an efficient hire.

Top performers who have worked for you in prior companies are great hires. You know their strengths and weaknesses, how they are best managed, and if they will be a cultural fit with your new company. There are numerous people that have worked for me on multiple occasions at multiple companies throughout my career. When I was at a new company and a new position opened up, if one of the top performers from one of my prior positions was a good fit I would contact them to recruit them for that open position at my new company.

Be sure that your job is posted internally within your own company. If you have a more entry-level type of role that you need to fill, it may open up the opportunity for someone in a different department to transfer as a part of their own career path. I have done this successfully in the past, although it is very important that you establish an open line of communication with the person's current manager. Everything should be done transparently so that a void isn't created in another area of the company.

Most companies have an employee referral program to incent employees to refer candidates for open positions. Once a position is posted, you may also receive applications from employees in other departments wanting to move into sales.

Don't be left hanging. Make sure you are continually using all of these tactics and others of your own to continually develop an ongoing talent pool.

What is your strategy for developing an ongoing talent pool?

Section IV
Optimizing

Inside sales teams are constantly evolving. These are the rules that will keep you and your team on top of your game and consistently delivering results.

34 Optimize Lead Conversion

The simple act of placing a phone call to a new prospect within a minute of lead generation can increase your likelihood of conversion by nearly four hundred percent.

According to The Ultimate Contact Strategy, a sales optimization study performed by Velocify, "The simple act of placing a phone call to a new prospect within a minute of lead generation can increase your likelihood of conversion by nearly four hundred percent."

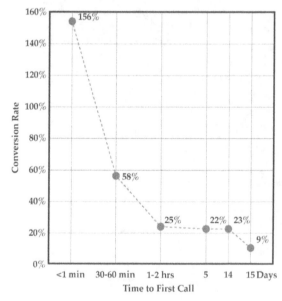

Source: Velocify, The Ultimate Contact Strategy: How to Best Use Phone and Email for Contact and Conversion Success.

As you can see from the figure above, each minute a rep waits to contact a prospect greatly reduces their chance of converting the prospect.

We were brought in to a company after they had missed revenue targets for several quarters. This resulted in their reducing marketing expenses and company layoffs—a common action companies take when revenue targets are missed. Ironically, this only made the problem worse. Sales still did not have enough leads.

We found that hundreds of highly qualified leads from company webinars had not been contacted for months. Using a typical conversion rate and average deal size, this equated to nearly $500,000 in lost revenue. Had these leads been contacted in a timely manner—enabled by best practices—the company would have made their revenue targets and avoided the associated reductions.

Another factor in optimizing lead conversion rates is the number of attempts made to follow up with the lead. In the same aforementioned study, Velocify stated that, "Shockingly, ... 50 percent of leads are never called a second time." They found that "93 percent of all converted leads are reached by the sixth call attempt."[44]

Combining follow-up calls with emails at properly timed intervals gives a company the maximum chance of converting valuable and difficult-to-generate inbound leads. The figure below, also part of the Velocify study, outlines this strategy, which can improve conversion rates by 128 percent.

The use of texting can lead to conversion gains of over one hundred percent if used properly, according to Velocify. "The content, timing, and number of texts should be dictated by actions taken by a prospect and by the prospect's status in the process. [...] Sending three or more purposeful text messages after contact has been made with a prospect can increase conversion rates by 328 percent."[45] Do not send text messages prior to making contact with a prospect—it can negatively impact lead conversion rates.

How quickly will your team follow up on their leads?

---

[44] The Ultimate Contact Strategy: How to Best Use Phone and Email for Contact and Conversion Success., http://pages.velocify.com/UltimateContactStrategy.html.

[45] Velocify, "Text Messaging for Optimized Enrollment" (enrollment optimization study), *Velocify*, September 1, 2013. http://pages.velocify.com/rs/leads360/images/Sending-Text-Messages-Prospect-Edu.pdf.

35 Appreciate the Value of Time Management

In setting up a new inside sales team, it is important to coach your team with the proper time-management techniques.

Along with the physical location(s) of the team members (Rule 6), you need to plan for reps to be available to buyers and customers during the times that they are most readily available to take a call. This seems paradoxical in today's electronic world when people may generally be available, yet have become more difficult for a sales person to reach.

In a geographic coverage model, your reps assigned to a geographical area should be "virtual" to that time zone and work the business hours that make the most sense for their buyers.

For example, ABC Company is a small company located in San Francisco. The core hours for their rep working the Eastern U.S. would be 6:00 a.m. to 3:00 p.m. PST. This would cover 9:00 a.m. to 6:00 p.m. EST.

If you have chosen a round-robin approach to lead management, all time zones need to be considered. If domestic (U.S.-only), then shifts may be as early as 5:00 a.m. to 2:00 p.m. to as late as 10:00 a.m. to 6:00 p.m. (These are defined as core hours because successful sales professionals do not work on the clock and there will be times when an event alters this schedule.)

To maximize productivity, consider time management at an individual level. While the core job is contacting potential customers and prospects, other activities must be addressed each day. For example, research may be required prior to outreach. These activities should occur during the slower periods of the day. Another option is to have a separate role called a lead researcher (Rule 4).

Consider Cathy who arrives at 8:00 a.m. She prepared for her day last night and is ready to start calling her top leads list from 8:00 a.m. to 10:00 a.m.

Then she moves to a schedule like the sample below, prospecting for new leads before and after lunch and reserving the early afternoon for work on more time-consuming custom emails and voicemails. Late afternoon includes a meeting, admin work, and prep for the next day before returning to her top prospects list.

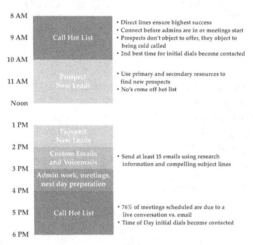

Source: Source: Vorsight, Outbound Prospecting Best Practices: A Day in the Life of a Vorsight Rep.

We can't stress enough the importance of reps preparing for the next day the night before. So much productivity can be wasted in the morning getting coffee, chatting, and reading email.

According to Laurie Lacey, Manager, Global Marketing Operations HPSW Lead Management,

> I conducted an experiment with two reps at an enterprise application company. The experiment was to have my top rep stay off email in the morning and provide her mobile to customers for urgent matters. I also took a low-producing rep and had them stay out of email in the morning and provide their mobile number. Both reps' activity and pipeline increased by 15 percent.[46]

In setting up a new inside sales team, it is important to coach your team with the proper time-management techniques to deal efficiently with these responsibilities and distractions.

What does time management look like for your team?

---

[46] Laurie Lacey, email message to Lori Harmon, October 8, 2013.

36 Combine Inside Sales with Internet Sales

Combining Internet sales with an inside sales team can be a powerful combination that expands the products sold online.

Many companies offer products that can be purchased online and downloaded. A sales rep is often not required to complete the sale. However, in some cases, combining Internet sales with an inside sales team can be a powerful combination that expands the products sold online. The approach is most effective and commonly used for retail products or technology products with lower price points.

One company where I worked had a powerful machine for lead generation—online sales and inside sales follow-up. The marketing programs drove thousands of prospects to the website where they could purchase the product. When clients made their initial purchase, their contact information was captured. This information was funneled directly into a contact management system for the reps to utilize in their outreach. This project was implemented prior to the creation of predictive dialers and the expected daily call volume was one hundred calls per day.

The reps attempted contacting the customer within minutes of making a purchase. The purpose was to upsell the customer on additional licenses and products. An email from the CRM was automatically sent to the customer providing upsell and contact information. They also provided an online chat service to answer questions during and after a purchase.

The company felt these methods added value and generated more revenue for the company, but found it difficult to measure the actual contribution by inside sales reps.

Team assignments were changed from territory-based to round robin. An imaginary rep was added to the team to compare their performance to that of a live rep. We found only a fraction of live reps performed better than the imaginary rep. Because the impact of the live rep was minimal, we decided to move the team to a lower-cost location so that we could realize more profit using this approach.

A "chat" sales rep is an inside sales rep that sells using online chat technology. Retail stores frequently use this type of sales approach since it allows a rep to maintain multiple chats with multiple prospects at the same time. If you have the volume to justify dedicated chat reps, it makes sense for them to either only use chat or be assigned to chat for certain periods of time on a daily or weekly basis. If it is only certain periods of the day, productivity may be impacted by having to switch back and forth or they may miss return phone calls from prospects while they are assigned to chat.

Consider combining inside chat sales reps with Internet sales. This does not mean they can't call or accept a call from a prospect that they are selling to; rather, their primary communication with prospects is via chat technology. If this is an acceptable and preferred buying method for your prospects, it is a highly productive approach to combining inside sales and Internet sales.

Internet sales can be highly lucrative for a company. It is not a substitute, however, for the intuitive ability of a sales person to identify buyer behavior, the potential for future purchases, and/or long-term commitment. A personal touch is the key to generating upsell opportunities.

What steps will you take to combine inside sales and Internet sales?

37 Perform Call Monitoring and Coaching on a Regular Basis

Monitoring should cover all forms of employee communication with the buyer: calls, emails, and chats.

Call monitoring and coaching is one of the best ways to ensure the effectiveness of your sales reps. Other benefits of listening to calls and providing constructive feedback include: increased sales, rapid identification of problems and operational obstacles, improved employee engagement, and a better prospect or customer experience.

There are two ways to monitor the calls of your inside sales reps: recorded and live.

Performing the monitoring from a recorded version may be less intimidating for the inside sales rep but it is also likely to be less effective. Unless you role-play a revised version of the call when giving them feedback after the fact, the rep does not get an opportunity to try the new skills you are asking him or her to learn. Reps are unlikely to want to try a new skill for the first time with a prospective buyer.

Real-time monitoring enables you to coach the rep during the call, allowing them to make real-time adjustments and see how the improvements play out with their prospective buyer. In this scenario, the coach and the rep, are both on the call. The coach will debrief with the rep at the end of the call using a standard template (Appendix E). This will improve the success of the call that they are currently making and enable them to get comfortable using the new skill the coach is teaching them.

I coached a rep recently that would never leave a voicemail or send an email per the best practices defined in Rule 34. I explained to her that if you never leave some type of message, you will never get a response. She began sending emails when she did not reach a person live. She got responses, which ultimately lead to more meetings.

Monitoring should cover all forms of employee communication with the buyer: calls, emails, and chats. What if a rep had perfect phone skills but was derailing their success with the emails they were sending? Not only does the messaging on emails need to be reviewed, but many times coaching is needed around grammar and even making sure they are properly using spell check.

When monitoring your employees, make sure they are getting positive feedback along with feedback on how they can improve. If you only focus on the improvement portions, the process will be very demotivating.

There is no specific guideline to the frequency of performing call monitoring. It depends upon the number of reps that a manager has and their level of experience. When a junior rep is ramping up within the company, you want to monitor their communication weekly. If the rep is more senior with a proven track record of success, then monthly will suffice. If you have a superstar on your team, you may even consider using them as a mentor or supplemental coach.

It is common for your inside sales reps to be uncomfortable with their calls being monitored, especially when done real-time. It is important to listen to their objections and address them. You can assure them that this is a standard process for any inside sales team and that everyone on the team is being monitored. Also, explain how this process benefits them and the entire team. This ongoing feedback helps them to become a better, more successful sales person. Reviewing different call scenarios in a training session helps the entire team improve.

Using a standard template to provide input gives you and the individual rep a record that shows their strengths and weaknesses and allows you both to track progress. These can also be saved as input to their annual performance review.

What will you do to coach and mentor your team?

38 Gear Your Training to Inside Sales

The activities of inside sales reps are still differentiated from that of outside sales reps and, therefore, they require training that is relevant to their position and how they need to operate to be successful.

"I understand inside sales well enough to know that they are tired of training sessions geared for outside sales." –Josiane Feigon, President, TeleSmart Communications.[47]

Just as inside sales requires specialized management skills, they also require specialized training. The activities of inside sales reps are still differentiated from that of outside sales reps and, therefore, they require training that is relevant to their position and how they need to operate to be successful.

TeleSmart offers a 10-step training program customized for inside sales. We have listed the 10 steps here to give you an idea of why it is so critical to customize your inside sales training to inside sales. Details of the TeleSmart 10 are covered in Josiane's bestselling book *Smart Selling on the Phone and Online.*[48]

- **Time Management**
  Inside sales is about time, how you plan it, and use it to your advantage. Time management is so critical that we have an entire rule (Rule 35) on the topic.

- **Introducing**
  Inside sales averages 40 to 75 calls and emails per day, trying to achieve a connect rate of 8

---

[47] Josiane Chriqui Feigon, *Smart Selling on the Phone and Online: Inside Sales That Gets Results* (New York: AMACOM, 2009).
[48] Ibid.

percent to 10 percent. You have four seconds to make a good impression with an email and seven to 15 seconds on a call. This requires selling in sound bites.

- **Navigating**
  Every sales rep has to identify the power buyer and find the invisible lines of power in a company.

- **Questioning**
  Today's buyers have lost patience with sales rep's questions. When you are on the phone, it is critical to understand how to effectively and efficiently question the buyer to get the information required to build trust and identify real opportunities.

- **Listening**
  It is easy to get distracted when you are on the phone. Yet actively listening to your buyer's answers to your strategic questions is the only way to understand their real pain.

- **Power Linking**
  It can be uncomfortable to call on a C-level decision maker when you are an inside sales rep. Having the confidence to call high and knowing the language to use to establish credibility and value are key skills for inside sales reps that need to sell at the executive level.

- **Presenting**
  Inside sales uses the latest Sales 2.0 technology platforms (like web conferencing) to make presentations. These presentations have to be compelling to hold the attention of your buyers.

- **Handling Objections**
  Sales reps always encounter objections from buyers and have to know the best way to handle them and keep the sale moving forward.

- **Closing and Gaining Commitment**
  Accurate forecasting is key to your credibility as a sales rep. Knowing which deals are going to close and how to close them gives you the ability to deliver an accurate forecast to management.

- **Partnering**
  As we state in Rule 40, it is a company-wide effort. Today, inside sales is an integral part of the sales process and, in many cases, the only sales team for the company. They must take a leadership with the company-wide team throughout the sales process.

Once you have selected or designed a training program that is geared specifically for an inside sales team, remember that training is not a one-time event. Effective training requires repetition, reinforcement, coaching, and accountability on an ongoing basis.

How will you gear your training to your inside sales team?

39 Create a Culture of Communication and Feedback

Communication takes work and practice. Feedback allows you to gauge the effectiveness of the communication.

"To effectively communicate, we must realize that we are all different in the way we perceive the world and use this understanding as a guide to our communication with others."[49]—Anthony Robbins

Effective communication in any company is an essential part of the corporate culture. If employees do not feel empowered to speak up and share ideas, they can easily become disengaged. If this happens for extended periods of time, your organization may get an unfavorable reputation that impacts your ability to keep and retain top talent.

Communication takes work and practice. Feedback allows you to gauge the effectiveness of the communication. The inside sales manager needs to stay alert to both verbal and nonverbal forms of communication at all times. In meetings, this includes encouraging the team to participate in discussions and to actively listen. As a communicator, the manager should keep the messages positive when possible. Obviously, if a team misses their targeted quota that is not a positive message. It is important to recognize both verbal and nonverbal cues as feedback.

It is critical that inside sales managers articulate and demonstrate that they have an open-door

---

[49]"Anthony Robbins," Wikiquote, last modified January 10, 2013 (1:24 p.m.), http://www.goodreads.com/quotes/152284-to-effectively-communicate-we-must-realize-that-we-are-all.

policy. They should not just sit in their office; they should be visible to their team by walking around and actively engaging.

In meetings, it is especially important to set proper expectations by asking an inside sales rep to confirm their understanding. During annual reviews, there should be no surprises if you have good ongoing communications.

One way we improved communications was by creating a program called "Food for Thought," which included lunch and a brainstorming session focused on how we could improve. This went beyond simply listening to issues that may already exist and be obstacles to selling. This was a session to encourage reps to think outside the box about actions we could take going forward to dramatically improve what we were doing.

Each month a group of six to eight reps were invited to participate in the Food for Thought session. We wanted to keep the groups small so that each person would have an opportunity to contribute and feel more comfortable in a more intimate group. Reps from different inside sales teams were selected to get a cross-section of input. Attendance was tracked so that we could ensure everyone had the opportunity to participate at some point during the year.

Everyone's suggestions would be noted. We selected the top three items on which to take action. I followed up with a summary of the discussion and listed those items. Each month I sent a status update on the steps taken to move the top three initiatives forward. Even if we ran into obstacles completing these initiatives, employees knew we were listening and taking action on items that were important to them. By seeing the forward progress, they became comfortable in regularly communicating more ideas.

Both reps and the company benefited from these sessions. In one instance, we increased the lead contact rate from 40 percent to 90 percent by implementing a change to our CRM system, giving reps faster and better visibility to marketing generated leads.

What steps will you take to encourage open communication and feedback?

40 It Is a Company-Wide Effort

A successful inside sales team needs support from all departments.

Sales is a corporate function connected to all others. While sales is a customer to other departments, the results generated by sales pay the bills, including everyone's salaries. No one department can be successful by standing alone. A successful inside sales team needs support from all departments.

Marketing and inside sales should work very closely together. Your inside sales team will be tied to marketing's demand-generation program and sales enablement tools. While metrics on lead follow-up will be captured in your CRM, it is highly recommended that the teams meet regularly. Marketing can advise the inside team on the talking points to use when following up on upcoming events and programs, and on new sales enablement tools being developed. In turn, the inside sales reps can provide feedback and valuable subjective information to help make adjustments to future demand-generation programs.

Product marketing has the responsibility of training sales on new products, buyer personas, and use cases. If product marketing is off the mark, sales success is impacted by wasting time trying to sell to the wrong buyers or because they do not have a sufficient understanding of the new products.

While inside sales may not work as closely with product development, they are on the front line. If a certain feature is lacking, then the team can relay that back to the product management team who sets the development priorities. Product development may also get involved if a prospect is requesting a specialized or unique solution.

Your inside sales team works with people in finance on several fronts. The finance department will need to be consulted if non-standard credit or payment terms are needed for a new customer. They are ultimately responsible for calculating and making sure that commissions are accurate and paid on time.

Another team or person that will likely be supporting your inside sales efforts is the legal staff. In the B2B world in particular, contracts are the norm. Despite everyone's best efforts, there is generally always a back-and-forth on terms, especially when it involves large opportunities and big corporations.

Human Resources has the responsibility of rapidly recruiting inside sales reps that are both qualified and are a cultural fit. They are part of the on boarding process for new hires, making sure the reps are comfortable with important compensation elements like medical benefits. If there is a performance or policy violation problem with a rep, Human Resources gets involved.

When a significant sales win takes place, make sure that it is broadcast to the widest appropriate audience, maybe the whole company or perhaps just a division of the corporation. Be humble in acknowledging contributions that others in the organization made to the efforts. Remember, it is a team in the broadest sense and as much as people are there to support the sales team, they also deserve recognition for a job well done. There may have been a sales operations person that went above and beyond the call of duty or perhaps a renewals sales rep that uncovered an opportunity and passed it to an inside sales team member as a lead. Perhaps there was an employee in finance who rushed a credit-check to help close a deal by quarter end. Being humble will take you far because you never know when you are going to be in a pinch and need help again.

What will you do to ensure alignment with the other functional areas?

Be Willing to Adjust

Ensuring your inside sales team continues to be a high-velocity team requires being open and willing to make changes.

Inside sales has evolved rapidly over the last 20 years and will continue to change along with the market, technology, buyer behavior, and more. Nothing in life stays static. Consider the explosive growth of social media over the past few years. Many of those who started their career with the advent of inside sales are now struggling to catch up to the new technologies that have become essential parts of a business person's tool belt.

This is why it is critical for inside sales leaders to stay current with upcoming trends. This means getting out of your office, networking, attending conferences, and reading the latest books and articles. While keeping your own skills and knowledge current, you are also setting an example to your inside sales team that they should be doing the same.

This is also one of the reasons metrics are so crucial. You may start with a set of metrics that gets optimized. Your team is a machine and they are on fire, blowing through their numbers! Then, it stops working. Why? It is likely that some external factor(s) has/have changed. If you are consistently monitoring your metrics you will see them start to drop off before there is a big crash and will have the opportunity to adjust.

Of course, you don't have to wait for a change in your metrics. If you are following this rule and staying current with industry trends and staying abreast of your buyer behavior, you can institute change proactively. You can get and stay ahead of the curve and be a leading-edge manager.

Another key way to know what changes need to be made is to listen to your reps. Reps are the ones on the front lines, talking to prospects and customers every day. During your weekly meeting, one of the agenda items should be "opportunities for improvement." Find out what steps you and the company can take to eliminate barriers for your reps and help them accelerate the sales process. If training is needed—by you or the reps—seriously consider making the investment.

One company where I worked required a huge adjustment with their inside sales team. Due to a favorable market, the inside sales team had been outrageously successful, in some cases closing deals as large at $200,000. Unfortunately, the market changed and the economy became significantly tougher. This inside sales team went from not being able to keep up with the number of deals they were closing, to not being able to close a deal. The company did not have any products at price points under $50,000.

After evaluating the situation, it became clear that a significant adjustment was required. If the team could no longer close deals, what should their role be? Outside sales was now closing all of the deals and they had no pipeline; this team had to be repurposed into a sales development team. Understandably, the individual reps were not happy and a lot or turnover was anticipated and did occur. However, it was the right decision for the company. Within three months we had built a significant pipeline for outside sales, which was what they needed to be successful in producing the company's revenue targets.

Ensuring your inside sales team continues to be a high-velocity team requires being open and willing to make changes.

What steps will you take to make the necessary adjustments to keep pace with change?

42

These Are My Rules. What Are Yours?

We would love to hear from you about what rules you have broken and what new rules developed during the building of your high-velocity inside sales team(s).

The rules in this book are based on our collective 40-plus years of experience in building, leading, and selling for high-velocity inside sales teams. Not all rules apply all of the time or to every situation. Each company should develop a solution that is appropriate for their business objectives, customer base, and product set.

We would love to hear from you about what rules you have broken and what new rules developed during the building of your high-velocity inside sales team(s). Please contact us via any of the following channels:

info@quantum-sale.com

www.quantum-sale.com/blog

www.linkedin.com/company/quantum-sale

@quantumsale

We hope you found the information in this book valuable. We hope that you now have a successful high-velocity inside sales team. Feel free to let us know if you need any assistance or clarification.

Glossary

AA-ISP – membership group, American Association of Inside Sales Professionals

B2B – business to business

B2C – business to consumer

cold lead – a person or entity who has never heard of your company or product

committed deal – an opportunity that is expected to close with a specified degree of certainty

CRM – customer relationship management, typically a term used to define methodologies and software that companies use to manage and organize customer relationships

hot lead – a prospect who has a need that your product/service can address

lead – a person or an company that has the potential to purchase a product or service

lead rating – a status typically assigned by a marketing automation tool to distinguish the lead's quality and prioritization

lead status – a progression of a lead from origin until it is passed as Sales Qualified Lead (SQL)

local presence – appearing, in the case by telephone identification, that you are local to the person whom you are having an interaction

MQL – Marketing Qualified Lead

OEM – Original Equipment Manufacturer

opportunity – an actionable and criteria qualified lead

pipeline – a representation of opportunities and steps that define your sales process

power dialer – an automated phone dialing software or application that is typically integrated into the CRM tool

prospect – a potential customer who has expressed an interest in your company's product or service

qualified lead – a potential customer (prospect) who has expressed interest in a product or service and has met general buying criteria.

rules of engagement – rules that define the circumstances and manner in which Inside and Outside sales interact, especially with regards to the customer

sales funnel – a graphical representation of the sales cycle

SaaS – software as a service, generally referred to as a product that is cloud based

SDR – sales development representative

SPIFF – Special Pay Incentives for Fast Sales

SQL – Sales Qualified Lead

upside deal – an opportunity that has the potential to close with a specified degree of certainty

VAR – Value Added Reseller

warm lead – a prospect who has heard of or has a recollection of you product and/or company

Expert Resources

Here are some of "expert" resources that I referenced in Rule 5. It is not complete as I am learning and finding new ones almost daily.

Membership Groups

- AA-ISP – American Association of Inside Sales Professionals

LinkedIn Groups

- Inside Sales Association
- Inside Sales Experts
- Inside Sales Managers
- Sales 2.0 Best Practices

Blogs

- Kenkrogue.com
- blog.bridgegroupinc.com
- marketing.vorsight.com
- salesbuzz.com
- mrinsidesales.com/insidesalestrainingblog/
- tele-smart.com/blog

B Onboarding Sample Schedule

Part 1

- New Employee Orientation: Human Resources - Ideally,this would be first so that the new hire could start the day filling out forms and securing IDs
- Logistics: computer, phone, workplace set-up
- Facility Tour
- Organizational and Key Contacts: inside sales manager or sales VP and key contacts in other functional areas
- Company Overview and Positioning: CEO or other senior executive

Lunch is a great way to welcome a new hire. It could be with a manager or a peer who might be identified as a sponsor.

- Buyer Personas, Buying Behaviors, and Case Studies: product marketing
- Value proposition and Business Solution Review: product marketing
- Product Positioning and Competitive Overview: product marketing

Part 2

- Product Pricing: product marketing
- Product Demonstration (if applicable): product marketing
- Charter and Objectives of Position (sales development rep, inside sales): inside sales manager
- Sales Methodology: inside sales manager
- The Sales Model and Process: inside sales manager

- Lead Qualification Criteria and Process: inside sales manager
- Pre-call Planning and Research: inside sales manager
- Activity Metrics Expectations and Compensation: inside sales manager
- Review Call and Email Templates and Usage: inside sales manager
- Handling Objections: product marketing

Part 3

- How to Do a Deal: inside sales manager and sales operations
- Forecasting Methodology: inside sales manager or sales operations
- RFP/RFI Process (if applicable): inside sales manager or sales operations
- Leveraging Partners (if applicable): channel manager
- Territory/Account Plan Development: inside sales manager
- Resource Utilization: inside sales manager
- Tools Usage: inside sales manager or sales operations
- Time Management: inside sales manager
- Marketing Calendar and Social Media Activities: marketing
- Role-Play: scenarios established and monitored by inside sales manager
- Creating an Individual Success Plan

Appendix

C Productivity Metrics

As I stated in Rule 15, metrics are needed to monitor business activities and make adjustments where necessary. Listed are examples of metrics commonly used in evaluating the effectiveness of your inside sales team.

Quantitative:

- Number of Leads by Source– the total number of leads coming into your company and from where they originated

- Number of Opportunities – the total number of opportunities in your sales funnel

- Amount of Closed Business – the dollar value of the business that has been closed

- Sales Forecast – the estimated amount of business that will be closed in a specified timeframe

- Deal Velocity – the rate in days in which an opportunity moves through the sales process.

- Number of Calls (Outbound versus Inbound)— as discussed in Rule 13, if you have a predictive dialer, calls can easily exceed one hundred per day. The number of calls is also dependent on how much additional research needs to be done prior to making a call. In a B2B world, with no predictive dialer, 50-60 calls per day is a good rule of thumb.

- Number of Connects/Contact Ratio—this will be dependent upon who you're trying to reach. Based upon my experience, calls to busy B2B executives can be at the 10 percent connect rate, while for real estate agents it can exceed 40 percent.

- Time to Contact: this enables understanding if your reps are adhering to or able to keep up with industry best practices contact timeframes (Rule 34). If not, lead conversion rates will not be optimized.

- Talk Time

- Number of Emails: this is very hard to measure—it's tied into call volume metrics, as some prospects/customers are easier to reach than others by phone.

- Number of MQLs: this is a count of the number of MQLs generated by marketing and passed to sales.

- Number of SQLs: shows the total number of sales qualified leads/ meetings, the number generated by each rep, and the marketing campaign source of the lead.

- Pipeline Contribution: shows the total dollar value of the pipeline contribution made by the SDR team and by individual reps.

- Conversion Ratios: shows the conversion ratio of connections to SQLs, SQLs accepted or converted to pipeline opportunities and to each stage in the sales process, and the number of SQLs not accepted or converted by Sales.

- Lead/Opportunity Aging: how long a lead has been open for SDRs and Sales, opportunity aging or number of days an opportunity has been in each sales stage.

Qualitative:

- Lost Deal Reasons: the reasons deals are lost captured in your CRM.

- Lead Status: shows progression of leads through the SDR process from marketing qualified lead (MQL) to sales qualified lead (SQL).

- Lead Rating: compares the MQL rating to the SDR rating to determine the accuracy of the score generated from the marketing automation system

- Lead Activity: shows the activity level against leads and the level of effort required for an SDR to move a lead from MQL to SQL.

- Lead Quality: summarizes the information about the lead captured during the lead qualification process.

- Forecast Accuracy: see Rule 26.

- Closed Business Source: from SDR passed SQLs, by inside and/or outside sales rep, by marketing campaign source, new versus installed base.

D Social Media

In Rule 23, social media was discussed. The following information can be used as a reference on how to extend your (inside) sales team's efforts in today's changing sales environment. I have included the most common social media platforms currently being used by inside sales.

LinkedIn

• LinkedIn is crucial for business networking. LinkedIn Premium allows sales people to message potential business contacts and warm up a cold call. It also shows sales people who in their network may have a contact at a company where they are looking to break through. LinkedIn is the best tool for sales people to utilize.

Facebook

• Facebook is a great way for sales teams to follow the companies who they are trying to engage and learn about their values and brand. Sales people are able to message brand pages and that can help turn a cold call warm. Plus, Facebook business pages consistently share causes and ideas which will give the sales person topics that can be used to connect with prospects.

Twitter

- Twitter is also a great way to understand a company's values and focus. Sales people can follow their leads or potential customers on Twitter to help understand them better and to connect on topics. Twitter also allows people to tweet to or direct message brands and other Twitter users in order to try to make a sales contact. Sales people can also follow industry experts, relevant hash tags, and businesses on Twitter, helping them to understand the industry they are selling into and better serve their customers.

Google+

- Similar to Facebook and Twitter, Google+ is a tool for understanding the industry where you are selling your product or service. Sales people can follow relevant industry leaders, brands, plus past and current contacts. However, Google+ is far smaller than Facebook and Twitter so the contacts made there will be limited.[50]

---

[50] Jenna Green, email message to Lori Harmon, October 18, 2013.

Phone Call Coaching Tips

1. While on the call, listen and take notes.

2. After the call, let the rep debrief the call, then review the following:

   - Introduction
   - Rapport
   - Listening
   - Questioning
   - Overcoming Objections
   - Presenting
   - Closing - sale or next steps

3. Summarize recommendations and move onto next call.

About the Authors

Lori Harmon, CEO of Quantum Sale, helps companies make quantum improvements in their sales results.

Lori is a veteran high-tech executive with more than 25 years of strategic and operational experience in all major functional areas, including sales, support, and marketing for some of Silicon Valley's leading companies. Her expertise lies in building and simplifying organizations, inspiring and developing high-performance management teams, and streamlining operations.

Lori has a keen ability to understand complex business issues, make solid recommendations, and quickly implement solutions that deliver results.

Since 1995, she has been leading inside sales teams, starting at Network General, where she built the inside sales team and grew the revenue from $0 to $50 million in two years. Since then she has led inside sales teams at Brio Software, Interwoven, and VeriSign.

Lori exudes amazing acumen in the sales arena like no other in her field. She is able to assess the flaws in any sales process and determine the exact remedy. Results include reduced cycle times of 20 percent+ and increases in revenue and productivity from 16 percent to 300 percent.

Prior to Quantum Sale, Lori was Executive Vice President of Global Partner Solutions at Melbourne IT, providing online services to Enterprises for resell to small businesses. During her tenure at Melbourne IT, Lori used her sales and overall operational experience to bring in new business and expand the product offerings.

Prior to Melbourne IT, Lori was Vice President and General Manager of the Digital Brand Management Services business unit at VeriSign. As the leader of this $30 million, 130-person business unit, she leveraged her extensive experience to develop innovative initiatives to enhance products and services for enterprise clients.

Originally, Lori joined VeriSign as Director of Worldwide Sales Operations, and quickly advanced to Vice President of Inside Sales and Worldwide Sales Operations before moving to an expanded role as Vice President of Global Customer Support. Her broad experience and ability to create value for the organization resulted in her promotion to General Manager.

Prior to VeriSign, Lori held senior management positions at Interwoven, Brio, and Network General leading inside sales, product marketing, and professional services organizations. Ms. Harmon holds a BS degree in Information Systems from Appalachian State University.

Debbi Funk is currently Vice President of Operations and a sales consultant for Quantum Sale.

Debbi has over 20 years of sales experience as a top-performing individual contributor and as an effective inside sales manager. She specializes in pipeline development, process improvement, and leading teams to achieve exceptional results.

Prior to joining Quantum Sale, Debbi was Manager of Sales Development at VeriSign, where she led a team that was an initial point of contact for representing primarily security products and services to prospects and customers. Her successes included hiring, training, and mentoring top talent into the organization. Her collaborative approach allowed her to be a liaison between the sales and marketing teams to optimize the results of both.

Prior to VeriSign, Debbi held various sales and management positions at Software Development Technologies, Brio Software (now part of Oracle), Network General, Telogy, and Everex Systems. Debbi holds a Bachelor's degree in Marketing from Santa Clara University.

42 Rules Program

A lot of people would like to write a book, but only a few actually do. Finding a publisher and distributing and marketing the book are challenges that prevent even the most ambitious authors from getting started.

If you want to be a successful author, we'll provide you the tools to help make it happen. Start today by completing a book proposal at our website http://42rules.com/write/.

For more information, e-mail info@superstarpress.com or call 408-257-3000.

Other Happy About Books

Increase Sales Effectiveness

42 Rules to Increase Sales Effectiveness (2nd Edition) is a highly readable guide containing the key fundamental tools and concepts that apply to professional selling and personal sales effectiveness.

Paperback: $19.95
eBook: $11.45

Turn Prospects

This book provides a practical step-by-step guide on how to find the right prospects, build profitable relationships, sell for success, and close more sales.

Paperback: $19.95
eBook: $14.95

B2B Social Media

The authors explain how to understand market requirements, engage in conversations with your customers, build awareness for your solutions, and generate targeted leads.

Paperback: $19.95
eBook: $14.95

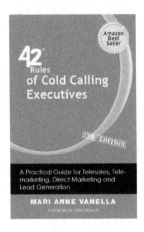

Cold Calling

'42 Rules of Cold Calling Executives (2nd Edition)' is an easy to read book that gives concise, easy to implement methods to get results with cold calls.

Paperback: $19.95
eBook: $14.95

Purchase these books at Happy About
http://happyabout.com/
or at other online and physical bookstores.

A Message From Super Star Press™

Thank you for your purchase of this 42 Rules Series book. It is available online at: http://www.happyabout.com/42rules/superiorfieldservice.php or at other online and physical bookstores. To learn more about contributing to books in the 42 Rules series, check out http://superstarpress.com.

Please contact us for quantity discounts at sales@superstarpress.com.

If you want to be informed by email of upcoming books, please email bookupdate@superstarpress.com.